Backcountry Cuisine

Tasty Meals for Off Grid Dining

Valerie L. Askren

Backcountry Cuisine
Tasty Meals for Off Grid Dining

Published by 42nd Parallel, LLC. While not off grid, we can be reached at HiketheBluegrass@gmail.com. If you have any suggestions on improving the book, catch any errors or have any updates, drop us a line!

ISBN 978-1-7378156-0-0

Printed in the United States of America. First edition.

All photos are by the author, with the exception of those generously shared by friends and family. All contributors retain all rights to their photos. *Thanks everyone!*

For those who love to eat well,
on and off the trail.

Contents

Introduction .... *x*

Tips, Tricks and Techniques *1*

Breaking Fast

Breakfast Tacos *17*
Vegetarian Breakfast Burrito *18*
Spicy Sausage Scramble *19*
Hash Browns *20*
Sweet Potato Hash *21*
Easy Potatoes O'Brien with Sausage *22*
Home–made Potatoes O'Brien with Soysage *23*
Country Ham or Sausage, Biscuits and Gravy *24*
Egg Nest Quiches *25*
Fruit–n–Nut Pancakes *26*
Cornmeal Pancakes *27*
Banana Bread (Fruit & Nut Bread) *28*
Cinnamon or French Toast *29*
Creamy Rice Pudding *30*
Goatmeal *31*
Trail Yogurt *32*
Breakfast Smoothies *33*
    Elvis's Favorite
    Very Berry
    Trail Tropical
    Green Goddess
Chocolate Chip Chickpea Bars *34*
Cherry Hazelnut Bars *35*
Komar's Bars *36*
Tasty Breakfast Hacks *37*

Lunches, Soups and Salads

Spicy Sesame Peanut Noodles.................................... *41*
Vegetable Yellow Curry.................................... *42*
Tuna Wasabi Mash.................................... *43*
Shiitake Udon Noodles.................................... *44*
Easy–Peasy Pizza.................................... *45*
Couscous with Mix–ins.................................... *46*
Colcannon.................................... *47*
Salmon Chowder.................................... *48*
Coconut Curry Coup.................................... *49*
Creamy Lentil.................................... *50*
Roasted Red Pepper and Pear Soup.................................... *51*
Single–serving 'Instant' Soups.................................... *52*
    Cream of Cauliflower
    Cream of Mushroom
    Cream of Peanut
    Broccoli Chowder
Lemony White Bean and Tuna Salad.................................... *53*
Mediterranean Chickpea Salad.................................... *54*
Asian Somen Salad.................................... *55*
Carrot–Pineapple Salad.................................... *56*
Napa Slaw.................................... *57*
Waldorf Salad.................................... *58*
Gingered Apple–Zucchini Salad.................................... *59*
Wakame Seaweed Salad.................................... *60*
Miso Veggie Salad.................................... *61*
Southwest Bean Salad.................................... *62*
Wild Rice Salad with Apples and Pecans.................................... *63*
Chicken Curry Salad.................................... *64*
Tasty Lunch Hacks.................................... *65*

Sides and Small Plates

Guacamole.......... *69*
Hummus.......... *70*
Baba Ganoush.......... *71*
Salsa Roja.......... *72*
Salsa Verde.......... *73*
Mango Salsa.......... *74*
Refried Beans.......... *75*
Spaghetti or Pizza Sauce.......... *76*
Gravies.......... *77*
    Beef or Chicken
    Vegan
Spicy Cashew Queso.......... *78*
Cheese Sauce.......... *79*
    Real Cheese Sauce
    Freeze-dried or Powdered Cheese Sauces
Tofu Jerky.......... *80*
Salmon Jerky.......... *81*
Pesto.......... *82*
Kimchi.......... *83*
BrocCauli Bake.......... *84*
Artichoke and Sweet Pepper Fritters.......... *85*
Savory Corn Cakes.......... *86*
Corn Custard.......... *87*
Southwest Baked Beans.......... *88*
Roasted Veggies.......... *89*
Bannock (Scottish Skillet Bread).......... *90*
Chapatis.......... *91*
Cornbread.......... *92*
Corn Tortillas.......... *93*

Dinners and other Feasts

Chicken and Broccoli with Sun–dried Tomatoes........... *97*
Salmon Orzo in Lemon Garlic Sauce........... *98*
Smoked Sausage and Cabbage........... *99*
Mushroom Stroganoff........... *100*
Black Bean Burgers........... *101*
Salmon Burgers........... *102*
Tuna Burgers........... *103*
Mini Mountain Meatloaf........... *104*
Spaghetti and Mushroom Balls........... *105*
Chicken and Dumplings........... *106*
Beef Filet Mignon........... *107*
Creamy Grits Country–Girl Style........... *108*
Southern Comfort........... *109*
Creamy Vegan Tofu Pasta........... *110*
African Peanut Stew........... *111*
Cuban Picadillo........... *112*
Corn and Black Bean Quesadillas........... *113*
Street Tacos........... *114*
Tamale Pie........... *115*
Spinach and Mushroom Enchiladas........... *116*
Chicken Enchiladas........... *117*
Pizza and Calzones........... *118*
Chicken Tikka Masala........... *120*
Panang Curry with Peanut Sauce........... *121*
Tahini and Lemon–Ginger Noodles........... *122*
Pad Thai........... *123*
Sushi Maki, Temaki and Poké Bowls........... *124*
Favorite Homemade One–Pots........... *126*
Tasty Dinner Hacks........... *127*

Sweet Endings

Black Forest Pudding *131*
Gluten-free Chocolate Molten Lava Cakes *132*
Gluten-free Apple Muffins *133*
Strawberry Rhubarb Crunch *134*
Angel Food Fruit Compote *135*
Chow Mein Cherry Clusters *136*
Apple Caramel Crisp *137*
Tiramisu *138*
Peanut Butter Cream Pie *139*
Key Lime Pie *140*
Grand Portage Mud Pie *141*
Grasshopper Pie *142*
Lemon Meringue Pie *143*
Ginger Cheesecake *144*
Bananas Flambé *145*
Royal Chocolate Golden Lion *146*
(Almost) Nanaimo Bars *147*
Free Range Fruitcake *148*
Strawberry Spoon Cake *149*
No-Bake Cookies *150*
Sweet Mango Custard *151*
Avocado Black Bean Brownies *152*
Tasty Dessert Hacks *153*

About the Author *154*

Introduction

Yes, food does taste better outdoors—particularly after a strenuous day of physical activity. But we've also had a few really bad meals out on the trail. That Shepherd's Pie on the Grand Canyon was definitely yuck. And we sorely remember that night in the Wind River Range of Wyoming when it was our turn to cook and someone (me!) accidentally kicked over the pot of shrimp and grits. Oh, and there was that dark, cold night we dropped an entire pot of lasagna into the sand. All of those incidents resulted in a weight–loss program none of us were looking for.

But there are also lots of great memories of how good food can save the day, such as the week–long canoe trip on the Missinaibi River in northern Ontario. Our friends, They Who Must Not Be Named, preferred to not share meals and take turns cooking. So every meal we feasted, while they sat quietly with their simple, repetitious fare. One evening after several days of rain, river currents that always ran uphill, and continuous swarms of unrelenting mosquitoes, the sun broke out of hiding and we broke out our backpacker's oven. Being able to share warm, crusty home–made pizza made everyone's moods lift sky high.

We will never forget the smile on another friend's face when we pulled partially–frozen fillet mignon steaks out of our packs for a shared supper in the Porcupine Mountains along Lake Superior. *Hey Kyle. How would you like your steak done?* Nor the kiddo's grins in the Boundary Waters Canoe Area of northern Minnesota when we discovered an extra bag of chocolate pudding mix, the perfect pre–breakfast treat. Or after the cook misread a recipe that required 1½ cups water (*not* 11 one–half cups of water), and our supplementary spice box salvaged what could have been a disaster of a dinner.

Our friends and family also bring 'backpacking' foods while sailboat cruising, such as the San Juan Islands just north of Seattle or the British Virgin Islands of the Caribbean. In both regions, grocery stores can be scarce. Bringing along our own shelf–stable meals allows us to eat better and sail longer before needing to restock. The same is true for base–camping during rock–climbing trips or when planning for an extended, self–supported bicycle touring. Tasty, healthy light–weight foods can go anywhere!

We're also kinda' cheap and somewhat arrogant when it comes to our food. We don't like spending money on something that we can make at home that tastes better and for less money. Many outdoors people are also an independent bunch that crave self–sufficiency; risk-taking is in our DNA and experimenting on sustenance can be a risky, yet rewarding adventure. Discovering new backpacking or lightweight recipes is fun for us and might be for you too.

We really can't remember personally buying pre–made backpacking food, although years ago REI did send us a few free samples along with my order. We were so impressed with how far the quality had advanced. Freeze–dried foods have been a miracle for backpacking cuisine! So we're not suggesting you totally buck ready–made backpacking foods, but seriously consider making some of your own.

Notably, there are a few backpacking cookbooks and some good websites already out there. But in addition to recipes, we think what is equally important is sharing some insights for getting better food into your pack and down to your belly. That way you can continue creating and re–imagining what good trail food should taste like.

So how is this book laid out? Part 1 includes some important tips, tricks and techniques that we have discovered after years of making and eating backcountry foods. Recipes are great, but understanding the techniques allow you to create your own lightweight meals. There are also a few ingredients that you might be unfamiliar with, such as NIDO and ghee, which can turn good recipes into great ones.

The second part of the book includes lots of ideas for breaking fast in the morning, keeping in mind that breakfast is good any time of the day. Part 3 covers quick lunches, while Part 4 is a collection of sides and small plates that can complement many meals, such as salsas, sauces, and breads. Dinner and other feasts are covered in Part 5, followed up by 'sweet endings' to finish your day. Each section also includes a list of tasty hacks that will give you lots of great ideas to quickly pull a meal together from ready–made grocery items, without needing a recipe.

Meal definitions are mostly a matter of time and complexity. If a recipe can turn out a decent meal in a short amount of time we call it 'lunch'. If the meal takes longer to rehydrate and/or cook, we call it 'dinner'. But, don't be caught up in the nomenclature. Serving sizes are also hard to estimate. For example, if hash browns are your only dish for breakfast you might eat a lot. But if you're also having bacon and a fruit smoothie on the side, portions are going to change. Planning on dessert after dinner? Then your entrée portions might be smaller. Finally, your age, weight, rate of metabolism, and expected level of activity all influence how much you eat. Importantly, most recipes can be easily scaled up or down as needed. You may want to test the recipe first before taking it out on the trail to make sure seasonings and servings are right for you.

What about special diets and preferences? For many recipes we include suggestions as to how to make a meal, for example, vegetarian. Or gluten–free. Or more or less spicy. The same is true for amounts—if you really like rosemary, double the recommended amount. Hate cilantro? You can easily omit that soap taste. Feel free to experiment and substitute.

Recipes are simply suggested road maps. Don't be afraid to wander off–trail and find your own path to good food. So let's go!

Tips, Tricks and Techniques

On a hike, the days pass with the wind, the sun, the stars;
movement is powered by a belly full of food and water ...
– Ken Ilgunas

Meal Selection

Always think variety out on the trail in terms of foods, but also cooking times and complexity. Make French toast when the sun is shining and eat granola bars when you're packing up in the rain. If it's been a 60–mile day on the gravel bike, break out that pasta and chocolate bar for dinner. Save the other more complicated and time–consuming dinners for other nights. Doing an overnighter? Yeah, go for that beef filet. But also be practical. You don't want every meal out on the trail to be a 5–course extravaganza.

Many backpackers claim that lunch planning is the most difficult meal of all. Yes, that 5–pound sack of gorp, dutifully alternated with beef jerky, really gets tiresome at lunchtime. So be sure to give serious consideration to having a quick, cooked lunch (or two) out on the trail.

What about shared meals? If you trust your backcountry partners, sharing meals can be great. Personally we have found that individual breakfasts and lunches, combined with shared dinners, work well. That way you can take turns cooking the evening meal and plan something a little more group friendly like a big pot of chili or jambalaya.

In addition, evaluate bulkiness when meal planning. There seems to be a general trade-off between light and bulky foods versus heavy and compact. That bear can or food bag sure fills up fast!

A week–long foray at 6,000 feet? Then nutrient–dense, space, and weight are critical considerations. If you're really counting calories for a thru–hike, you will need to do a lot more meal planning than what this book provides. But use the tips and recipes for guidance and inspiration.

Finally, don't be intimidated by any of these recipes. If you're not a cook, that's okay. Start simple, try out a few recipes before you hit the trail, then one–up me by making them even better to suit *your* tastes. Experiment! Don't like walnuts? Substitute pecans. Vegetarian or Vegan? No problem—omit the chicken, use vegetable bullion for beef, and coconut oil instead of ghee. Think color. Black beans with a bright splash of red pepper. Think presentation. Take your pocket knife and add a few chocolate curls to that cheesecake. Think flexibility. There's something innately satisfying having leftover pizza for breakfast and omelets for dinner.

Recipe Jargon

The following recipes use typical cookbook jargon and units of measurement. For example, T = tablespoon and t = teaspoon. If you're not sure about any cooking terms in particular, google them or ask your partner.

Lots of the recipes are for 1 or 2 servings. But you can easily scale them up for your party (and pot) size. Look for on–line calculators if you want to convert lots of teaspoons to tablespoons, or tablespoons to cups.

Ingredients

Most of the ingredients used in these recipes are things found in your own home kitchen or easily purchased locally. But there may be a few items new to you.

Coconut cream or milk powder: Both can be purchased in most Asian grocery stores or on–line. Typically cream has a higher fat content than milk powder. However, the fat content is not always labeled and frequently these powders are interchangeable. Sometimes you can substitute NIDO (see below) but you loose that subtle, creamy coconut flavor. And of course, coconut powders are the go–to creamers for many Vegans.

Ghee: Ghee is cow's butter that has been heated low and slow, then strained to remove all the milk solids, including caseins and whey. It's cooked a step further than clarified butter, which gives it a golden color and nutty flavor. Ghee does not have to be refrigerated and is a solid at room temperature. However, in warm conditions Ghee can melt, so be careful storing it outdoors. In most recipes, oil (including coconut oil) can be substituted for ghee. Look for ghee on your grocers shelf.

NIDO: NIDO is a full cream milk powder made by Nestlé. You can substitute regular (low–fat) powdered milk, but the lack of fat content, thus rich taste, will be noticeable. You can find NIDO in the grocery, next to the milk powders. It can be stored in your freezer to extend shelf life. NIDO is also good used in coffee.

OvaEasy: Powdered eggs have taken a backseat to high–tech egg crystals from OvaEasy. For baking recipes, powdered eggs still work and are cheaper. But for fresh–tasting scrambled eggs, OvaEasy is the way to go. You simply mix 2 parts egg mix with 3 parts cold water by volume. The following recipes make allowances for the amount of liquid needed to reconstitute the eggs (that is, you don't need to add extra water to the recipe.) OvaEasy is easily found on–line, but hard to find locally.

Single–serving packets: If you need an excuse to go to a fast–food restaurant this is it. Any place with carry–out food will frequently have a great selection of condiments that are the perfect size for the backcountry. And the nicer the restaurant (or country club) the nicer the condiments (from Grey Poupon mustard to lavender honey). Even some gas stations have a surprisingly good array of single–serving packets.

True Lime and True Lemon: These instant powders are the essence of their namesakes. They are a little hard to find locally, but can be easily sourced on–line. Be careful and only buy the boxes of packets—the 'shakers' include lots of other junk you don't want to eat. The recipes indicate the suggested number of packets, but if you really like things zesty, go for more.

Storage of 'Home–Made' Backcountry Food

Baggies: Most backpacking foods can be stored in baggies—but it's best to use freezer baggies as they hold up better and more easily reused. Take a Sharpie (permanent marker) and label by writing directly on the baggie. You want to have as little excess trash and bulk out on the trail as possible, so remove all excess packaging and consolidate ingredients as much as possible. (Why have 6 envelopes of hot chocolate? Just put all the contents in one baggie and label.) If making a dish that requires more than one 'baggie' of ingredients, label each baggie, and then combine all of the bags for that meal into one larger bag. Organization is key.

Labeling: In addition to labeling what is in each bag or package, you can also write simple instructions directly on the package. Let's say you have 1 cup of rice in a baggie that needs to be cooked—label the bag as *'rice'* AND something like *'+1.5 c H_2O, 20 min'* (add 1½ cups of water; cook for 20 minutes). If the recipe is more complicated, type or write it out, and staple it to the top of the package or tuck inside the bag. That way each recipe is right where it needs to be. As backup, you can take a picture of the recipe with your phone (if you're bringing it along on the trail).

Long–term storage: It's best to put food in an air–tight container, properly labeled, in a cool, dark place. Anything with a high fat content (such as meats) should go in the freezer. See tips for storing dehydrated foods on page 7.

Carrying oils and liquids: For small amounts of oils and liquids, you can't beat the little Thermo Scientific Nalgene bottles (pictured). Some prescription pill bottles, with little gaskets, also work well.

Dehydrated Versus Freeze–Dried

What is the difference between dehydrated and freeze–dried? From a technical standpoint, freeze–drying removes 98% of the water in foods, while dehydrating removes about 80%, giving freeze–dried products a much longer shelf–life. Other advantages of freeze–dried foods include: slightly higher nutritional content; better color and flavor retention; and much faster rehydration times, particularly for meats.

The advantages of dehydrated foods include: can be done at home; less expensive; packs into a much smaller space; more durable on the trail; and flavors can be infused before dehydrating. For example, you can roast Brussels sprouts with fresh garlic, sea salt, and balsamic vinegar, dehydrate, and then rehydrate at camp. In general, dehydrated and freeze–dried foods can be used interchangeably in recipes, but it is extremely important to keep rehydration times and water requirements in mind as they can significantly vary.

Where can I buy freeze–dried foods? Not long ago, you could pretty much only buy these on–line, but now even major supermarkets carry freeze–dried fruits and vegetables. Northbay Trading Company is an excellent source for both freeze–dried and dehydrated fruits and veggies, including organics. Many local food co–ops carry Northbay items in their bulk section. Recently, Honeyberry started selling freeze–dried fruits on Etsy. Mountain House and Honeyville are both good sources for freeze–dried meats. Packit–Gourmet is another good option.

Dehydrating Foods

Do I have to buy a dehydrator? Nope. But after just a few backcountry trips it will pay for itself. Dehydrators come in a variety of sizes and prices. A few key points:

1) Buy a good brand such as Nesco that has a temperature control and a powerful fan (you can get one for less than $100). Excaliburs sure are nice, but they're also expensive. Buy what you can afford. A good dehydrator will last you for many years.

2) Buy extra non–stick mesh screens and fruit roll sheets the same diameter and shape as your dehydrator trays (pictured on the following page). The mesh and fruit–leather trays sit on the basic trays (for support) while dehydrating. Use the non–stick fruit roll–up trays for dehydrating high–liquid or soupy things like spaghetti sauce, guacamole and salsa.

3) Follow the manufacturer's directions, but generally fruits and vegetables should be dehydrated at 135°. Yes, you can dry fruits and veggies at higher temps (to speed things up), but you do have a loss in nutritional content. Meats, including fish and dishes made with meat (such as jambalaya), should be dehydrated at 160°.

Basic trays for thick, chunky foods

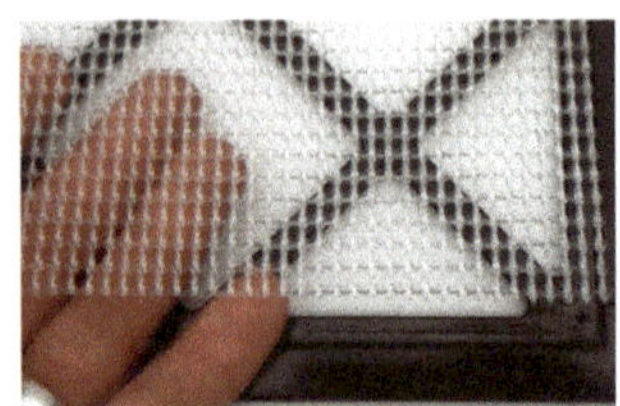

Mesh trays for fine foods

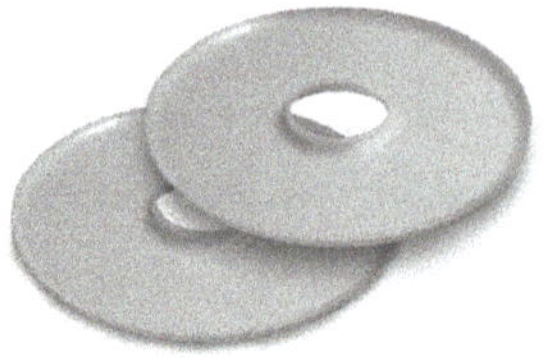

Fruit roll sheets for liquid foods

Dehydrating in bulk: Once you get that dehydrator out, crank it up! Don't just dehydrate one green pepper. Do red, yellow, orange, jalapeno, and pobalano. Mushrooms on sale? Perfect to dehydrate and store until needed. Too many apples? Thinly slice, toss in lemon juice, place on tray in single layers, then dehydrate. Making a pot of chili? Go ahead and dehydrate the leftovers for your next adventure.

Once you have a stash of dehydrated foods, it's easy to mix and match them for meals. Those yellow peppers pictured here are perfect to throw in the skillet for that morning omelet, used for pizza toppings, or tossed with other veggies for fajitas. The same holds true for mushrooms, onions or greens. Similarly, dehydrated fruits are perfect to snack on, mix in with your morning oatmeal, or add to puddings and other desserts.

Having a supply of dehydrated foods also makes it easier when someone calls at the last minute to do an overnighter. And for real backcountry foodies, a large bag of your dehydrated chicken creole could be the best birthday present ever.

More about dehydrating veggies: You can dehydrate fresh or processed vegetables. Toss your fresh veggies in a little lemon juice (or diluted vinegar) to improve color retention. Most canned and frozen veggies have been pre–treated so they don't brown as they dehydrate. You can also roast fresh vegetables and then dehydrate, as mentioned in the Brussels sprouts example earlier.

Again, this gives you the opportunity to infuse flavors before dehydrating. Either way, beginning with dry, warm veggies will speed up the dehydration process.

Making fruit leathers: Throw fresh or frozen fruit into a blender and puree on high to a smooth consistency. Spread evenly over the fruit roll–up tray. Dehydrate at 135° until it cracks on top. (Half–way through, you may want to peel if off and flip it over to dry on the other side.) Cool slightly, roll or fold, and store in the refrigerator or freezer. The same technique works for applesauce, spread directly from the jar.

More dehydrating tips:

- In general, pieces of uniform–size and thickness are best for even dehydration.
- Don't overfill trays, as it simply slows down the dehydration process.
- If you don't fill all trays, space the empties between the full ones for better air flow.
- After an hour or two, shuffle the positions of the trays for even heating and drying.
- Don't be afraid to flip pieces over to ensure even drying.
- Foods that easily turn brown such as apples, peaches, and mushrooms, can be tossed in lemon, lime, orange or pineapple juice (something acidic) to keep colors true. You will see that technique used in several of the recipes.
- Always use the basic tray as support underneath the mesh or fruit roll sheets.

Storing dehydrated foods: Do not place recently dehydrated foods into storage containers until they are completely dry and cool to the touch. If storing in baggies, be sure to remove all the air from the bag. You can also store dehydrated foods in canning jars, vacuum pack them, etc. In general, if foods are properly dried, they can be stored in an airtight container in a cool, dark place for at least a year. However, there is absolutely no harm in storing them in the freezer. This is particularly true for foods with a high fat content, including meats. Again, be sure to label clearly and date if you think they might be stored for any length of time. This bag of dried peppers is the same three yellow peppers shown on the facing page.

Why dehydrate cooked pasta and rice? Good question! There are two advantages: First, cooking pasta and rice first, and then dehydrating, significantly shortens cooking times at camp. Second, you can infuse flavors directly into the grain before dehydrating, enriching flavors significantly. (See the chicken curry and wild rice salad recipes as examples.) The downside to dehydrating cooked pasta and rice is it requires more upfront work and the final product is bulkier.

Rehydrating on the trail: If using dehydrated foods for every meal, you may need to plan ahead. The rule of thumb is to start rehydrating one meal ahead of when you want to eat. So at breakfast, start meal planning for that day. Some foods can be rehydrated using the freezer baggie you stored them in. But to be sure they are leak–proof, consider investing in some Nalgenes or Ziploc containers with screw lids. Ziploc Twist'n Locs are much cheaper and lighter, but the Nalgenes are much more durable. Either one are great for rehydrating your salads or dips for lunch.

For dinner, if you get into camp early enough it's easy to start dehydrating. If it's a dense food, such as chili, heat water in a pot and then add the dry mix. Turn off the heat, cover the pot tightly with a heavy rock on top, and store in a safe place. By the time you have set up your tent and inflated your sleeping pad, the miracle of applying heat to water will make you a rock star.

Trail storage: Obviously you need to keep your food cache dry and safe from critters. More and more wilderness areas and parks are requiring bear cans or vaults for food storage. Do a test run before you leave town to make sure all your food will be adequately protected. Fitting everything in can be a real challenge! But these bear cans also protect your food from getting crushed in your pack and make excellent stools. Even touring cyclists need to protect their food from bears and other varmints while in camp.

Kitchen Gear Extras

Most of you already have your favorite backpacking stove, fuel cannister, pot set and so forth. If not, you'll be overwhelmed with the reviews found on–line. These decisions are as personal as hiking boot selection and won't be addressed here. But we do have a few favorite kitchen items that can be lifesavers out in the backcountry.

Cutting board: Definitely a luxury item. But those really thin, plastic ones slide right into the back of your pack and come in handy if you need a relatively clean, flat surface to cut on, or to roll dough.

Pack towels: If you have nesting pots, take an old pack towel (that perhaps a chipmunk ate holes in), and cut circles the same inside diameter as each of your pots. Use these 'pads' between your pots to protect pans from scratching (particularly those with non–stick or ceramic finishes), to reduce rattling noises while moving, and for handy drying towels.

Mini silicone spatula: Yes, another luxury item. But they are terrific at keeping foods from sticking to the bottom of your pots and pans. They even make little, silicone–coated, wire whisks for your pudding and hot chocolate. Bamboo handles further save weight.

Spice Set: Some people swear on the value of bringing a small spice set on the trail. Tony Chachere's Creole Seasoning has saved many a dish. Lemon pepper seasoning if you're planning on fishing. Thyme, sea salt and ghee if foraging for mushrooms.... You get the idea.

Collapsible handles: The 'foldable' handles allow you to find room for cheese graters, serving spoons and spatulas. (Hint: cheese graters can also help drain pasta.) Just make sure the utensils have a locking mechanism so they don't collapse on you while cooking.

Obviously you don't need to bring everything, every time. And if you're shaving ounces, you might ditch all of these ideas!

Baking on the Trail

Baking in the backcountry is not as difficult as you might think. But it does require a little planning and can be fuel–intensive. Here are three different ways to make those baked goods we all love. For cupcakes and the like, consider a hot–water bath. For fresh–baked cornbread (crusty on the outside, moist on the inside) or authentic pizza, we love the Backpacker's Pantry Outback Oven, shown on the facing page. The last option, Banks Fry–Bake pan has it's own rewards.

For cupcakes, muffins, brownies: The secret is using *silicone* cups that can withstand heat to well over 400° F. Since water boils at 212° F, you can create a hot–water bath for your baked yummies. Inexpensive silicone cupcake liners and bowls are easily found both locally and on-line. Happily, these liners are re–usable, do not need paper liners or to be greased, and come in bright, cheery colors. But be forewarned, for some reason little critters like to nibble on these, so be sure to keep them safely stowed when not in use.

While some people bake in a dry pot, we prefer the hot water method. The technique is quite simple; mix your batter as desired and pour into liners. Place filled liners in your pot (large enough to hold however many cakes you want to make). Fill the pot with water so that the level reaches ½ to ⅔ of the way up the side of the filled liners. Place a tight–fitting lid on the pot.

Carefully place the pot over your stove and bring the water to a boil. Reduce to a rolling simmer. That's it! Baking times vary depending on the size of your liners and the mix itself. Just be sure to occasionally take a peak to make sure the water has not boiled out. The cupcakes or muffins are done if the top of the cake springs back lightly to the touch. Remove from heat and uncover the pot. Allow to cool until you can safely remove the liners from the hot water.

You can use this baking technique with any sweet cakes or savory breads. Although just–add–water mixes are easy, you can also measure out NIDO and OvaEasy to fulfill any milk and egg requirements.

What's a Backpacker's Pantry Outback Oven?: This is an amazing 'oven' that is no longer manufactured. We continue to search on eBay, Craig's List, FB Marketplace, used gear sites.... all to no avail. Yes, there are a few other similar products out there, but we love our backpackers oven—in fact we have two, one of each size. And no, we are not interested in selling either one. But drop me a line if *you* have one to sell! We only bring the oven along on special trips and then we try and use it for several meals.

The oven comes with: a skillet (with an extremely durable, non–stick finish); a tight–fitting lid with a somewhat unreliable thermostat; heat dome; heat diffuser; foil deflector; pot–grabber; cutting board (large size only); and mesh storage bag. The other major downside (beside being extremely hard to find) is that you need to use an external heat source such as an MSR WhisperLite stove and fuel bottle. Read the previous sentence twice.

There are some other backpacker oven hacks you can make yourself and some available for purchase, but we have yet to see anything that compares with our beloved. But if you Google something like 'backpacking oven' you will get several interesting hits, including YouTube videos that are fun to watch. Double–nesting pots or skillets is probably the simplest hack and makes good use of cookware that you probably already own.

So the next time you're out slurping cold ramen noodles and the unmistakable aroma of freshly–baked biscuits or cornbread slathered with ghee, deep–dish pizza topped with stringy mozzarella, or rich, chocolate brownies drifts your way, think about how you too could hack your very own backpacker's oven. It's best to practice at home first to make sure you know what you're doing, but have fun with it.

What about Banks Fry–Bake pans? Made of hard anodized aluminum, Fry–Bake pans are basically light–weight versions of a Dutch oven. The general idea is that you can bake by applying low heat under your pan, while applying a much hotter heat on the top, allowing the baked goods to rise.

Fry–Bake pans come in two different sizes: 8" wide and 1½" deep; and 10½" wide and 2" deep (weighing 12 and 29 ounces, respectively). This is a little on the heavy side for most backpackers, but quite reasonable for other outdoor chefs, for example while kayak or canoe camping.

Although these pans function as great skillets, their real beauty lies in their baking capabilities. The surface of the pans also accommodates metal utensils such as spatulas, and cleanup of the pan itself is fairly easy.

The downside of using these baking pans is that you must build a small twig fire or place coals on top of the lid while your goodies are baking. This leaves the lids rather sooty and more difficult to clean. And open fires are not always permissible in wilderness areas.

Finally, you really need some kind of tongs to arrange the coals or adjust the twig fire on top of the lid. This or another tool is also needed to lift the lid off the pan. More things equals more weight to carry.

The photos on the left give you a good idea of how these baking pans work—our dog Bear slept through the whole thing until it was time to scavenge the crumbs of the blueberry cake, made from an 8 ounce just–add–water muffin mix from Weisenberger Mills and the 8" Fry–Bake pan.

If you notice a blackening of your food in the bottom, you have your stove heat too high. If there's a darkening or burning on the top of your food, you have the lid fire too hot. But it doesn't take much practice to get this right. The basic baking process is as follows:

1) Pour a small amount of oil into the pan. Place pan on your stove over medium heat and distribute the oil evenly. (Note: Not all foods require oil.)

2) Pour your batter, casserole or dough into the pan.

3) Place the lid on top of the pan and cover with a small twig fire or hot coals.

4) Turn the heat on the stove down as low as it will go. Half-way through the baking process you can even turn the stove off and just use the heat from the fire or coals resting on the lid.

5) The muffin mix on the previous page took about 12 minutes to bake, using very little stove fuel. You can even use a few coals underneath your pan and skip using the stove all together. But this also gets the bottom of your baking pan sooty, meaning a little more cleanup.

6) To check if the baked goods are done, carefully move the fire aside and pick up the lid. Take a peak. If you smell anything burning, your lower heat is probably too high. Baked goods spring back to the touch and smell heavenly.

Whose turn is it for dishes?

Leave–no–trace practices require just that.... leaving no trace that you have been there or done that. If you're not familiar with the proper way to dispose of food particles and wash dishes, please see lnt.org or other respected sources for guidance. We are the first to admit—having Bear do the pre–rinse makes our lives much easier.

Breaking Fast

Expect problems and eat them for breakfast.

– Alfred A. Montapert

Breakfast Tacos

Hint: Dehydrate the guac and salsa in large batches to use in other recipes. You can also dehydrate your own sausage, but it will take longer to rehydrate than the freeze–dried.

1 serving (easy to adapt for multiple servings)

You'll need:
3 T freeze–dried sausage crumbles or two slices vacuum–packed pre–cooked bacon
2 T OvaEasy whole egg crystal
2 T dehydrated guacamole (page 69)
2 T dehydrated salsa (pages 72 – 74)
Ghee or oil
Two small or one medium corn or flour tortilla
Packets of hot sauce (optional)

At home:
Package meat in one baggie, egg crystals in another baggie, and the guac and salsa in a third. Package the ghee or oil and tortillas separately. Note: All of the vacuum–packed bacon should be used shortly after opening the package.

On the trail:
Add 3 T water to the egg crystals. Add enough water to the sausage and guac/salsa bag to saturate. Massage each bag to mix thoroughly. It will take about 15 minutes for everything to fully rehydrate. Heat ghee or oil in pan; add sausage or bacon. Slide to one side of pan, add ghee, and cook the eggs on the other side. Once done, cover with tortillas (to warm). Flip pan onto your plate and cover with toppings. Add hot sauce if you lean that way.

Vegetarian Breakfast Burrito

Hopefully you have stock–piled these basic ingredients and you're ready to roll! Servings can vary.

You'll need:
1 can black beans or vegetarian refried beans (page 75)
Dehydrated veggies (page 6)
Dehydrated guacamole (page 69)
Dehydrated salsa (pages 72 – 74)
Chunk of hard cheese or cheese stick
Tortillas

At home:
If using canned black beans, drain and rinse, then dehydrate on fine mesh tray at 135° until dry. Dehydrate veggies, guac and salsa. Bag all ingredients as needed.

On the trail:
Rehydrate beans and veggies with just enough water to cover for about 20 minutes. Throw everything into a pot (except for the cheese and tortillas), slowly heat, adding more water if necessary. Turn heat off and cover pot with tortillas to warm. Grate or slice cheese onto warm tortilla and scoop bean mixture on top. You're good to go!

Spicy Sausage Scramble

Hands down, one of our breakfast favorites!
2 small servings or 1 large

You'll need:
4 T OvaEasy whole egg crystal
4 T freeze–dried sausage crumbles
2 T chopped sun-dried tomatoes
1 T dehydrated spaghetti sauce (page 76)
½ t dried oregano
Pinch of cayenne (to taste)
1 T ghee or oil
1 or 2 T dried Parmesan or Romano cheese

At home:
Mix powdered eggs, sausage crumbles, sun–dried tomatoes, spaghetti sauce powder, oregano, and cayenne in a baggie. Pack the remaining ingredients separately. Note: The sun–dried tomatoes should not be the kind packed in oil. Plant–based 'sausage' crumbles can also be dehydrated in lieu of the sausage.

On the trail:
Add ½ to ⅔ cup water to the bag with the scramble mixture and mix well. Close the bag and set aside for 10–15 minutes. Melt the ghee or oil in a frying pan over medium–low heat. Pour in the egg mixture and let sit for about 20 seconds. Gently scramble until the eggs are softly set. Remove from the heat and sprinkle with cheese. This is also good wrapped in a tortilla.

Hash Browns

One cup of dehydrated hash browns, with peppers and onions, weighs only 1.2 ounces. These are also good used in stuffed breakfast burritos.

You have lots of options here:

You'll need at home:

1) Buy frozen hash browns and dehydrate them yourself. Thinly spread potatoes on fine mesh trays. Add chopped peppers, onions, or greens if desired. Dehydrate at about 135° for 2 to 3 hours, or until dry. Once cool, place in baggie.

2) Grate your own potatoes and toss with lemon juice to keep from browning. Thinly spread on mesh trays. Add chopped peppers, onions, or greens if desired. Dehydrate at about 135° for a few hours, or until dry. Once cool, place in baggie.

3) Buy hash browns that are already dehydrated. They come in what looks like those small milk cartons from kindergarten. Repackage using a small baggie.

Bring: Ghee or oil; packets of ketchup, hot sauce and/or creole seasoning.

On the trail:

Add just enough water to the bag of potatoes (and veggies if using) to lightly saturate—you don't want the potatoes 'wet'. Heat the ghee or oil in pan over medium–low heat. Spread spuds in hot pan; try not to stir until toasty on the bottom. Flip potatoes and cook until done. Season as desired.

Sweet Potato Hash

Beautiful colors and a healthy way to start your day.
2 large or 4 side servings

You'll need:
1 large or 2 medium sweet potatoes, diced
½ cup onion, any kind, diced
Fresh garlic, diced or minced
½ red pepper, diced
Large handful (or two) fresh spinach or kale, chopped
Salt or creole seasoning to taste
Olive oil
Packets of ketchup or hot sauce (optional)

At home:
Pour a small amount of oil into a skillet. Sauté onions and garlic until slightly soft. Add sweet potatoes. Cook until al dente. Add red pepper; cook until slightly soft. Toss in spinach or kale, and cook a minute or two more, until wilted. Season to taste. Dehydrate at 135° until dry. Cool and dump into baggies.

On the trail:
Add just enough water to bag or container to cover hash. Rehydrate for 3 to 4 hours (best done the night before). Reheat in skillet—no additional oil is needed.

Easy Potatoes O'Brien with Sausage

Super easy using store–bought potatoes and freeze–dried sausage crumbles.
4 large servings

You'll need:

1 large (28–ounce) bag of frozen Potatoes O'Brien
Salt, pepper or creole seasoning to taste
1 or 2 cups freeze–dried pork sausage crumbles
Oil or ghee
Packets of ketchup or hot sauce (optional)

At home:

Leave the frozen potatoes on the counter until room temperature. Season as needed. Dehydrate on fine mesh trays at 135° until dry (about 5 hours). This large bag of potatoes dehydrated down to 2 cups and weighs only 5.5 ounces! Once the potatoes are cool, combine with the sausage crumbles, and dump into baggies. Store in refrigerator or freezer until you're ready to use. Package the oil or ghee in a leak–proof container.

On the trail:

Add enough water to the bag of potatoes and sausage to cover. You want the potatoes moist but not wet. Rehydrate for 1 hour or less. Heat the oil or ghee in a skillet. Once hot, add the potatoes and sausage mixture. After everything has browned on the bottom, stir potatoes and brown again.

Home–made Potatoes O'Brien with Soysage

Make your own Potatoes O'Brien and add plant–based crumbles.
2 large servings

You'll need:

1 large or 2 medium Yukon Gold or red–skinned potatoes, cut into ½–inch cubes
1 onion, any kind, diced
1 green bell or poblano pepper, diced
Salt, pepper, garlic powder or creole seasoning to taste
1 cup plant–based 'sausage' crumbles, thawed (if frozen)
Oil or ghee
Packets of ketchup or hot sauce (optional)

At home:

Pour a small amount of oil into a skillet. Sauté onions until slightly soft. Add potatoes. Cook until al dente. Add peppers; cook until slightly soft. Season to taste. Combine the 'sausage' crumbles with the potatoes. Dehydrate on fine mesh trays at 135° until dry (about 5 hours). Cool and dump into baggies. Package the oil or ghee in a small leak–proof container.

On the trail:

Add water to the bag of potatoes and sausage mixture, to cover. You want the potatoes moist but not wet. Rehydrate for about 1 hour. Heat the oil or ghee in a skillet. Once hot, add the potatoes and sausage mixture. After everything has browned on the bottom, stir potatoes and brown again.

Country Ham or Sausage, Biscuits and Gravy

Vacuum–packed country ham requires no refrigeration.
2 large servings

You'll need:
1 package vacuum–packed country ham
1 package just–add–water biscuit mix
Gravy mix (see page 77)

At home:
Make your own gravy mix (if desired). Package the ghee separately.

On the trail:
Ham: Saute ham in skillet until nicely caramelized on the edges.

Gravy: Follow directions on page 77 for your gravy du jour.

Biscuits: For the biscuits, mix with water as directed. Cooking options:
1) Wrap dough around a stick and cook over a fire.
2) Plop biscuit mix in a skillet and make thick pancake–style biscuits.
3) Use a Fry–Bake pan or backpackers oven (pages 11 – 12).

For Sausage:
Instead of country ham, use freeze–dried sausage crumbles. Place in baggie and rehydrate at camp. After making the gravy, simply dump the reconstituted sausage in with the gravy. Serve over hot biscuits.

Egg Nest Quiches

Corn tortillas are harder to form, but when the eggs set up everything holds together beautifully.
1 serving

You'll need:
1 tortilla, street–taco size (corn or wheat flour)
1 T dehydrated sausage, soysage, or shelf–stable bacon
1 T hard cheese or cheese stick
1 T dehydrated veggies
1⁄4 t spice or herb of choice (curry, Cajun seasoning, rosemary and so forth)
3 T OvaEasy whole egg crystal
Silicon cupcake liners

At home:
Package the first 4 ingredients as needed. Pack the egg crystals, along with any herbs and spices you might want, in a separate baggie.

On the trail:
Combine the egg crystal with 4.5 T of water and mix well. Using a tortilla, form a bowl within your cupcake liner (pictured right). Begin layering from the bottom up: protein; cheese; and veggies (there is no need to rehydrate anything.) Slowly pour the liquid egg crystals over the top of everything.

Use the hot-water bath baking instructions on page 10. Bake until set (about 20 minutes) or a bit longer at higher elevations. Carefully remove from the pot.

Fruit-n-Nut Pancakes

Mix the batter right in the baggie; snip off the bottom corner and gently squeeze batter right into your pan.
2 large servings

You'll need:
1 small package (about 5.5 ounces) just–add–water pancake mix
1 cup freeze–dried raspberries or other fruit
¼ cup chopped pecans
Real maple syrup
Ghee or oil

At home:
Note: If using other mixes, combine with NIDO and OvaEasy per instructions, place in baggie, and label with water requirements. Place fruit and nuts in second baggie. Syrup can be purchased in a pouch or poured into a plastic Nalgene or airline bottle.

On the trail:
Follow the directions on the pancake mix. Heat ghee or oil over medium-low heat. Add pancake batter and dot with fruit and nuts. Flip once bubbles form in batter or cakes are beginning to brown on bottom. Top with syrup. Other good combinations are freeze–dried bananas and walnuts, or freeze–dried blueberries and almonds.

Cornmeal Pancakes

A hearty breakfast when you're not in a hurry.
3 to 4 servings

You'll need:
1 cup cornmeal
1 cup all–purpose flour or gluten–free baking mix
1 T sugar
1 T baking powder
1 t salt
4 T OvaEasy whole egg crystal
4 T NIDO or coconut milk powder
¼ cup oil + extra oil for frying
Real maple syrup

At home:
Mix dry ingredients and place in baggie. Pack oil and maple syrup separately.

On the trail:
Pour 1½ cups water + ¼ cup oil into the baggie of dry mix and gently massage. Let rest for 10 minutes; add additional water if the batter is too thick. Heat pan with extra oil. Cut corner off baggie and squeeze batter into pan for cakes. Cook over medium–low heat. Flip once bubbles form in batter or cakes are beginning to brown on bottom. Serve with maple syrup.

Banana Bread (Fruit & Nut Bread)

Mix everything in the same baggie to make for easy clean–up; the hot–water bath makes it simple to bake. You can also substitute gluten–free baking mix for the flour.
3 to 4 servings

You'll need:

½ cup all-purpose flour
¼ cup OvaEasy whole egg crystal
½ cup sugar
1 t baking powder
1 cup freeze–dried bananas, in pieces
½ cup coconut or canola oil
½ cup almond flour (meal)
½ cup instant oats
1 t ground cinnamon
¼ t of salt
⅓ cup chopped walnuts
Silicone bowls or cupcake baking liners

At home:

You can use any kind of fruit or nuts. Mango and pecans? Peach and almond slivers? Yum. Just mix all dry ingredients together and put the oil in a separate bag or container. Coconut oil has a melting temperature of 78⁰, so plan accordingly.

On the trail:

Combine dry ingredients, canola or liquid coconut oil, and 2 cups of water. Mix well, but do not over stir. Let sit for about 5 minutes. Spoon into silicone cups or bowls. Use the hot-water bath baking instructions on page 10. These take about 20 minutes to bake until set, or a bit longer at higher elevations. Remove carefully from the pot.

Cinnamon or French Toast

Pocket pitas or naan pack well and work great for French toast.

You'll need:
Thick, fluffy tortillas, pita or naan
Cinnamon and sugar
Ghee or oil
OvaEasy whole egg crystal (optional)
Maple syrup or dried fruit (optional)

At home:
Mix 1 part cinnamon to 4 parts sugar. Place in baggie. Package other items as needed.

On the trail:
Heat ghee in pot or pan large enough to hold your carbs. Cut or tear tortillas or pita into fourths or sixths. Toast lightly, until heated through. While still warm, toss pieces in the cinnamon and sugar baggie to coat. That's it!

For French Toast: To eat like a Parisian, dip bread in OvaEasy liquid (reconstituted) egg first, then fry in a lightly–oiled pan. If you're not sure of proportions, it's 2 T of OvaEasy crystals to 3 T water. While the toast is still warm, sprinkle with cinnamon and sugar, real maple syrup, or rehydrated fruit. Ooh la la.

Creamy Rice Pudding

A nice change of pace from oatmeal. Use a sharpie to mark directly on the baggie how much water to add.
2 large servings

You'll need:
1¼ cups instant white or brown rice
¼ cup full cream milk powder (NIDO)
1 T OvaEasy whole egg crystal
¼ cup brown sugar
½ t cinnamon
⅛ t salt
⅓ cup raisins

At home:
Put all ingredients into one baggie. Honestly, instant rice is not the best, but it's fast and takes so little fuel. But if time and fuel conservation are not an issue, you may want to consider parboiled or regular rice. Short grain rice will give you the creamiest texture.

On the trail:
Boil 1½ cups water. Dump the entire contents of the baggie into the pot, stir well, place the lid back on the pot, and let sit for 5 minutes. Stir and taste. Let sit longer if needed. If using other than instant rice, follow the cooking instructions in terms of water and time required for cooking.

Goatmeal

The extra protein in this recipe will stay with you in the morning. It's also easy to scale up for bigger appetites, more people, or more days on the trail.
1 serving

You'll need:
⅓ cup freeze-dried fruit of your choice (mix or match)
⅓ cup instant or quick oats
1 T almond flour
1 T pecans, almonds or other nuts, chopped
2 T NIDO or coconut milk powder

At home:
Combine all the ingredients in one baggie. Mark on the bag how much water you will need. Dried fruits can also be used, but may take more water and longer to rehydrate.

On the trail:
Bring 1/2 cup water to a boil. Dump contents of baggie into pot. Stir. Turn off heat and let sit, covered, for 5 minutes.

Trail Yogurt

Dehydrated flavored yogurts make great snacks. Dehydrated plain (unflavored) or Greek yogurt can also be ground into a powder; after rehydrating, it can be used as sour cream out on the trail. Similarly, yogurt powders can be used in fruit smoothies (see the recipes on the facing page).

You'll need:
Yogurt, any kind, any flavor
For sour cream: Plain Greek yogurt

At home:
Very lightly oil (eg.,canola) a dehydrator fruit roll sheet. Spread yogurt evenly *or* place in quarter–sized drops on the sheet. One 6–ounce container of yogurt will fill up one sheet.

Dehydrate at 125° to 135° for about 6 hours. Remove from silicone sheet, flip, and dry another 6 hours until smooth and shiny. The yogurt will still be somewhat soft and pliable, similar to a fruit leather.

Once cool, place dried yogurt in a baggie. Store in the refrigerator until ready to use.

If making a powder for sour cream or smoothies, place the dehydrated yogurt in the freezer until crisp; then grind to a coarse powder in a small food processor. Empty the powder into a baggie and store in the refrigerator or freezer until ready to use.

On the trail:
Not much to do here, other than eat!

If dehydrating plain yogurt for sour cream, add a small amount of water to the baggie of powder. This should rehydrate rather quickly. Remember, you can also add more water if needed, so add the water sparingly at first.

Breakfast Smoothies

For a jump–start of a day.

Elvis's Favorite
1 T almond or peanut butter
1 banana
2 T wheat berries or rolled oats
1½ t cocoa
¾ cup almond milk

Very Berry
1 cup frozen mixed berries
1 banana
2 T wheat berries or rolled oats
⅔ cup orange juice

Trail Tropical
1 cup frozen mango or pineapple chunks
2 T rolled oats
2 T shredded coconut, unsweetened
¾ cup coconut milk

Green Goddess
1¼ cup unsweetened vanilla almond milk
1 apple, peeled and chopped
1 medium banana
1½ cups fresh spinach
½ avocado

For any of the smoothie recipes above:

At home:
Combine all the ingredients in a blender. Process at high speed until smooth. Spread on silicone fruit roll sheets. Dehydrate at 115° for about 6 hours until completely dry and brittle. Remove from dehydrator and freeze. Grind dried smoothie sheets into a fine powder. Pack in a small baggie. Store in freezer until ready to use. Alternately, you can also dehydrate and make into a fruit leather. Roll and go!

On the trail:
Pour smoothie powder into a mug. Add ⅔ to 1 cup water and stir well. Let stand for 5 to 10 minutes to rehydrate. Note: You can also mix this in your water bottle, but be sure to rinse thoroughly when finished.

Chocolate Chip Chickpea Bars

Make in advance for a quick and easy breakfast. Plus, they're excellent for bartering!

You'll need:

1 (15–ounce) can garbanzos or chickpeas, drained
½ cup all natural almond butter or peanut butter
⅓ cup pure maple syrup or honey
2 t vanilla
½ t salt
¼ t baking powder
¼ t baking soda
½ cup plus 2 T dark chocolate chips

At home:

Preheat oven to 350°. Lightly oil an 8x8 inch pan. In a food processor, add all of the ingredients, except the chocolate chips. Process until the batter is smooth. Fold in ½ cup of chocolate chips.

Spread batter evenly in the oiled pan; then sprinkle 2 T of chocolate chips on top. Bake for 20-25 minutes or until the edges are just starting to brown. The batter may look underdone, but you don't want them to dry out. Sprinkle with sea salt, if desired. Cool pan completely on wire rack before cutting.

To take on the trail, carefully cut into bars and individually wrap with waxed paper or plastic wrap. To prolong trail life, you can also freeze individual bars.

Cherry Hazelnut Bars

A raw bar for fast and long–lasting energy.

You'll need:
2 cups hazelnuts
2 cups Medjool dates
1 cup + ¼ cup dried (not freeze–dried) cherries
½ cup old fashioned or quick oats
½ t vanilla extract
½ t ground cinnamon
1 T unsweetened cocoa powder
⅛ tsp salt

At home:
In a large food processor, place all the ingredients, except for ¼ cup of the dried cherries. Grind until the mixture sticks together (not too crumbly, but not too gooey), for about 2 minutes. Add the remaining cherries and mix well.

Place the mixture in a lightly oiled pan, flattening and compressing as you go. Lining your pan with parchment paper or plastic wrap can help you remove the bars. Store in the refrigerator until needed. Since the fruit is dried, the bars will keep indefinitely.

Komar's Bars

Thanks Carolyn.

You'll need:

16 ounces of natural crunchy peanut butter
1½ cups honey
2¼ cups chocolate protein powder
3 cups old–fashioned oats (not instant oats)
Chopped nuts (optional)

At home:
Mix ingredients well in a large bowl. To aid mixing, you can slightly warm in the microwave. Smooth the mixture into a 9x12 baking dish and place in the refrigerator. When cool, cut into desired sizes and store either in the freezer or refrigerator. Recipe can easily be halved.

Tasty Breakfast Hacks

It's good to have a mixture of easy breakfasts for when you want to get on the trail early or the weather is just not conducive to cooking. Alternately, a hot and more time–consuming breakfast is great for a leisurely day in camp or for a slow start to your day. And remember, breakfast is always good for dinner, too.

- Granola, full cream milk powder (NIDO), and freeze–dried or dehydrated fruit.
- Just–add–water muffin mixes, made into pancakes. Even better with real maple syrup!
- Can of biscuits, divided, wrapped around the end of a stick, and cooked over a fire. Dust with cinnamon and sugar. Or use a can of 'cinnamon roll' breakfast rolls. It's amazing how many preservatives are in those things.
- Instant mashed potatoes with real bacon bits.
- Instant grits with cheese powder.
- Instant cream–of–wheat with brown sugar and raisins.
- Various instant oatmeal flavors with dried fruit, nuts, chocolate chips, Oreo crumbs.... Each morning you can create a whole new combination.
- Beef jerky and dried fruit, plus drink a whole lot of water to keep you regular.
- Tortilla, peanut butter, and shelf–stable bacon roll–up.
- For overnighters you can carry real eggs stored in plastic Easter eggs.
- Spam Single Classic and fried eggs (*whoa!*)

Lunches, Soups and Salads

Some weasel took the cork out of my lunch.

– W. C. Fields

Spicy Sesame Peanut Noodles

Add some freeze–dried broccoli for a splash of color.
2 servings

You'll need:
6 to 8 ounces thin spaghetti, ramen or other quick–cooking pasta
1 or 2 t crushed red pepper flakes (yes, it's spicy...)
2 T peanut butter powder
1 t garlic powder
¼ t ginger powder
½ t dried cilantro (optional)
2 packets True Lime
1 or 2 T soy sauce
1 t *toasted* sesame oil
1 T olive or canola oil

At home:
Place the pasta in a baggie. Mix all the dry ingredients in another baggie. Combine the liquid ingredients in a small leak–proof plastic bottle.

On the trail:
Cook pasta as needed. Drain water or use for rehydrating freeze–dried foods (see below). Add the liquid ingredients. Toss. Add dry ingredients and toss again. Let sit for a few minutes. Garnish with wild onions, if available.

For a fuller meal, add freeze–dried chicken and/or veggies, and crushed roasted peanuts. You can throw these into the same boiling water about half–way through your pasta cook time, but be sure to drain before adding the other ingredients.

Vegetable Yellow Curry

This is a mild curry, but the more curry you add, the stronger the kick!
1 large serving

Easy Method:

You'll need:
1½ cups *cooked* basmati or other rice (warm or room temperature)
1 T Thai yellow curry paste (or 1½ t dry curry powder, plus ⅛ t salt)
2 cups frozen vegetable mix, thawed (stir–fry veggie combos are good)
3 or 4 T coconut milk or cream powder (found in many Asian grocery stores)

At home:
Mix the cooked rice, veggies and curry paste together. Spread on dehydrator silicone mesh sheets. Dry at 135° for about 4 hours. Cool and add the coconut powder. Seal in a baggie. Using a Sharpie, mark the baggie with the water requirements.

On the trail:
Pour vegetable curry mixture into a pot; add 2 cups water. Place pot over medium heat and bring to a boil. Simmer, stirring occasionally, for about 5 minutes. Turn off heat, cover, and let stand another 5 to 10 minutes to fully rehydrate.

Even Easier Method:

You'll need:
¾ cup *instant* rice
1½ t dry curry powder
1½ cups freeze–dried vegetables
3 or 4 T coconut milk or cream powder
⅛ t salt

At home:
Mix everything well and store in a baggie.

On the trail:
Add the full contents of the baggie, plus 2 cups of water to your pot, and bring to a boil. Stir well, place the lid back on the pot, and let sit for about 5 minutes. Add more water and time if needed.

Tuna Wasabi Mash

A tasty way to increase your sodium intake.
2 servings

You'll need:
1 (4.1 ounce) package of instant potatoes (about 1 cup)
Small handful of dried seaweed (such as torn nori sheets or kombu)
1 t wasabi powder or more to taste (found at many Asian grocery stores)
2 to 4 packets soy sauce (or 2 T in a small leak-proof plastic bottle)
2 (2.6 ounces each) pouches tuna (lemon sesame and ginger is a fav)
1 T toasted sesame seeds

At home:
Mix instant potatoes, seaweed, and wasabi powder in a small baggie. Using a Sharpie, mark the baggie with the water requirements needed. Pack the remaining ingredients separately.

On the trail:
Bring 2 cups water to a boil. Add dry ingredients. Mix well. Top with tuna and soy sauce. Sprinkle with sesame seeds.

Shiitake Udon Noodles

Quick and easy to throw together, and to cook.
1 serving

You'll need:
3 ounces Udon noodles (or one 'bundle')
Small handful of dried shiitake mushrooms
1 packet instant miso soup (see note below)
1 T wakame or other seaweed (optional)
¼ to ½ block freeze–dried tofu (optional)

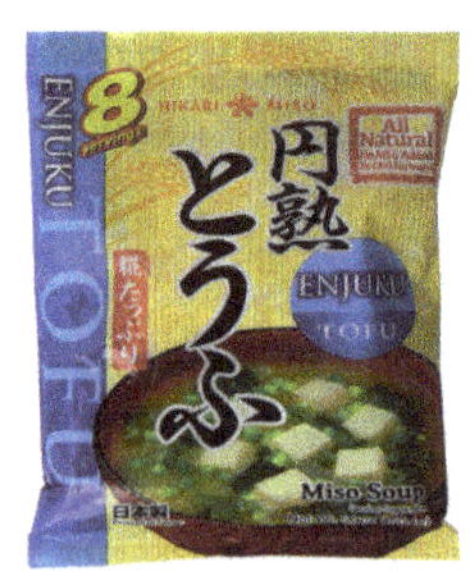

At home:
Either dehydrate mushrooms or purchase from any Asian grocery store. Combine all ingredients and place in a single baggie. Note: Some brands, such as Kikkoman, make an instant miso soup with teeny tiny pieces of tofu and seaweed already added. Freeze–dried tofu can be difficult to source locally and is NOT the same as dried tofu. Dried takes longer to rehydrate.

On the trail:
Soak shiitakes in a pot with 2 cups of warm water for 10 minutes or until soft. Add everything else to the pot. Add the lid; gently bring to a boil. Simmer for a few minutes and then let sit for a few minutes more. You can adjust the water required to make your noodles more or less 'soupy'.

Easy–Peasy Pizza

These personal pan pizzas make a fun lunch.
Make as many servings as you want.

You'll need:
Tortillas or naan the diameter of your pan or pot
Tube of double–concentrated tomato paste
Dried basil, oregano and garlic
Sliced or shredded provolone or mozzarella cheese
Sliced pepperoni, Sopressata or dry salami (optional)
Other toppings you like or want to experiment with
Packets of Parmesan and/or red pepper flakes

At home:
There's really not much to do! If you like thin crust pizza, use tortillas; for a slightly thicker crust, use naan. Store the herbs in a small plastic bottle or folded paper. The cheese will keep several days (depending on the weather), or you can freeze it before you leave home to extend its trail life. Peppers, artichokes, pineapple, capers, olives, etc. will also last a day or two in the backcountry.

On the trail:
Place tortilla or naan on bottom of non–stick or lightly–oiled pan or pot. Top with tomato paste, sprinkle with herbs and cheese, and whatever else you brought. Place lid on pan/pot and slowly heat through until bottom is a bit crusty, toppings are heated through, and cheese is gooey. Sprinkle with whatever. That's it! Mmm garlic naan....

Couscous with Mix–ins

Lots of different combos on this one. And couscous takes very little fuel to cook.
2 servings

You'll need:
1 (5.6–ounce) box couscous, any flavor (about 1 cup)
½ cup dried cranberries (or raisins, sun–dried tomatoes, etc.)
½ cups toasted cashews (or pecans, slivered almonds, pine nuts, etc.)
Optional: Dehydrated mushrooms, freeze–dried veggies or chicken

At home:
Remove couscous and spice pouch from box. Place in a baggie and write the water requirements on the bag with a permanent marker (usually 1 cup couscous to 1¼ cups water). Place cranberries and nuts in separate baggie. If you want this for multiple meals, grab different flavors of couscous and simply increase volume and variety of mix–ins.

On the trail:
Boil enough water for the couscous. If adding other veggies or chicken, increase the water accordingly. Add the couscous (and veggies and chicken if using), to the boiling water. Turn off heat, cover, and let sit for a few minutes to absorb the water. Stir in mix–ins.

Colcannon

A traditional Irish dish of mashed potatoes with cabbage, kale or other greens.
2 servings

You'll need:
2 cups of real instant potatoes, any flavor
2 or 3 cups of coarsely chopped cabbage, kale, leeks, chard, or other greens
3 green onions, sliced
Real bacon bits (optional)

At home:
Before dehydrating, swish your greens in watered–down lemon juice to help them retain their color. Dehydrate the greens and onions at 135° until dry, but still leathery (you want the greens whole and not dried to a powder.) After cooling, place in a baggie with the instant potatoes. If using leeks you may want to omit the green onions.

On the trail:
Bring 3 cups of water to boil. Dump everything in the pot, simmer for a few minutes, and then let sit for a few more minutes. Add more water as necessary to get the right consistency. Sprinkle with real bacon bits, if using.

Salmon Chowder

Instant potatoes make excellent soup thickeners.
4 servings

You'll need:
1½ cups freeze-dried corn and/or peas
2 T low–sodium chicken or veggie bouillon granules
1 cup instant mashed potatoes (any flavor)
½ cup full cream milk powder (NIDO)
2 (5–ounce) pouches of salmon (or more to taste)

At home:
Combine all ingredients into one baggie, except for the salmon.

On the trail:
Bring 6 cups water to a boil. Add the contents of the baggie, stir well, and simmer for just a few minutes—the freeze-dried veggies rehydrate quickly. Add salmon and heat thoroughly. Remove from heat and let sit for a few minutes to thicken.

Coconut Curry Coup

An easy soup to put together, with layers of rich flavor. (Is that title a typo or not?!)
1 hearty serving

You'll need:
1 or 2 t curry powder (see note below)
2 t powdered chicken or veggie bouillon
Pinch of cayenne (optional)
1 ounce (2 T) of coconut cream powder (found in Asian grocery stores)
3 ounces (80 grams) Pad-Thai rice noodles
1 cup freeze–dried cauliflower and/or broccoli

At home:
Combine coconut cream powder, bouillon and spices in a small baggie. Place noodles and veggies in another bag.

Note: You can use yellow curry powder off the spice aisle, or red or yellow curry paste that has been dehydrated at home. Either way, this soup is yummy. Curry powders really vary in intensity, so you may want to experiment a bit.

On the trail:
Place noodles and veggies in 2 cups water; simmer until tender (about 3 to 5 minutes). If using dried veggies, pre–soak or boil them first. Once noodles and veggies are soft, gently stir in the dry coconut cream mixture.

Noodles will expand as they cool. If you let the soup rest for five minutes, the layers of flavor become even more pronounced and mature.

Creamy Lentil

This same technique can be used for a variety of soups such as bean, split pea or vegetable. 4 to 6 servings

You'll need:

2 T olive oil
1 cup onion
1 cup chopped carrot
1 cup chopped celery
1 pound lentils (2 cups), any color, rinsed
7 cups chicken or vegetable stock
½ t each coriander; cumin; sea salt
¼ t each black pepper; cardamom; ginger

At home:

Heat the oil in a large pot. Add the chopped veggies and gently cook until tender (about 5 to 10 minutes). Add all the other ingredients. Simmer until lentils are soft. Red and yellow lentils cook in 15 to 20 minutes; green or brown take a bit longer. Let sit and correct seasonings if needed; stocks can really vary in saltiness.

Using an immersion blender or food processor, lightly blend into a thick soup. This will speed up dehydration time in camp, but you don't want to make baby food either. Alternately, you can skip this step, knowing the soup will take a little longer to rehydrate.

Dehydrate on silicone fruit roll sheets at 135° until dry. Cool and store portions in baggies.

On the trail:

Add the contents of the baggie to a pot and cover the soup with water. Rehydration times will vary from 10 to 30 minutes, depending on how finely you ground the stew. You may need to add more water. Just heat and eat!

Roasted Red Pepper and Pear Soup

Dehydrate as a fruit leather and rehydrate on the trial. This isn't just a recipe — it's a road map to making other delicious soups.
4 to 6 servings

You'll Need:

3 large red bell peppers
1 medium potato, chopped
2 carrots, chopped
2 t dried (not ground) thyme
Dash of cayenne (to taste)
1 medium yellow onion, diced
2 pears, cored, chopped
2 garlic cloves, minced
¼ t each salt and ground pepper
4 cups chicken or vegetable stock

At home:

Preheat the oven broiler to high, with the rack about 6 inches down. Lay the peppers on a cookie sheet and broil, turning frequently, until charred on all sides. Remove from oven and place in a paper bag until cool to the touch. Deseed and chop the peppers.

In a large pot over medium heat, add a small amount of oil. Cook the onions, potatoes, carrots, and garlic until tender and fragrant. Add the chopped peppers, pears, thyme, spices, and stock. Simmer for another 10 or 15 minutes. Adjust seasonings if necessary.

Remove from heat and cool. Using either an immersion blender or a food processor, blend until the consistency of applesauce. Pour the soup onto fruit roll sheets and dehydrate at 135⁰ until dry. Remove and tear into small pieces (to speed dehydration). Store in baggies.

On the trail:

Empty the soup baggie into a pot and add just enough water to cover. Heat on medium until steaming, then turn the stove off and let the soup sit (pot covered) until fully rehydrated. Add additional water and heat as needed.

Now that you understand the technique, you can make many other kinds of soup leathers! Parsnip and apple; cauliflower and broccoli; roasted asparagus; or spinach and kale?

Single-serving 'Instant' Soups

These amounts can be easily scaled up to make extra servings.
1 serving (heaping cup per person)

Cream of Cauliflower

3 T freeze–dried cauliflower
1½ T instant mashed potatoes, any flavor
1 T full cream milk powder (NIDO)
1 t chicken or veggie bouillon
1 to 2 T powdered cheddar cheese (optional)

Cream of Mushroom

2 T dried mushrooms
2 T instant mashed potatoes, any flavor
1½ T full cream milk powder (NIDO)
½ t dried thyme or rosemary

Cream of Peanut

2 T unsweetened peanut butter powder
1 T full cream milk powder (NIDO)
½ t chicken or veggie bouillon
½ t dried onion

Broccoli Chowder

3 T freeze–dried broccoli
1½ T instant mashed potatoes, any flavor
1 T full cream milk powder (NIDO)
1 t chicken or veggie bouillon
1 to 2 T powdered cheddar cheese (optional)

At home:
Mix all ingredients into a baggie.
With a Sharpie, write on the baggie the required amount of water (1 c H_2O).

On the trail:
Empty contents into a mug. Add one cup boiling water. Stir, cover and let soak 5 minutes. Add more dry instant potato flakes for a thicker soup.

Lemony White Bean and Tuna Salad

A new twist on an old Italian favorite.
2 large servings

You'll need:

2 (15–ounce) cans (about 3 cups cooked) cannelloni or white beans, drained
½ red onion, chopped
½ cup fresh greens (parsley, basil, oregano, kale etc. or any combo), chopped
Hot sauce or ⅛ t ground cayenne, to taste
Zest and juice of one large lemon (a microplane makes zesting a breeze)
2 pouches of tuna, (2.6 oz each), any flavor (but lemon pepper marries well)

At home:
Toss all ingredients together (except for the tuna) and, if you have the time, marinate for 4 to 8 hours or overnight. If needed, bring bean mixture to room temperature. Spread on dehydrator silicone mesh sheets. Dry at 135° for about 4 hours. Cool and seal in a baggie. Package tuna separately.

Interestingly, smaller white beans dry whole, while larger beans such as cannelloni tend to 'explode'. But they both rehydrate beautifully!

On the trail:
These beans take less than 45 minutes to rehydrate. If having for lunch, some time late morning fill the baggie with water to the top of the dry bean salad (not to the top of the baggie!) Place in a Nalgene or other plastic container with a tight–fitting screw lid. Store in your pack until ready to eat. Stir in the tuna packets just before serving.

Mediterranean Chickpea Salad

An easy salad to make ahead, but takes a long time to rehydrate.
2 very large servings

You'll need:
2 (15–ounce) cans (about 3 cups cooked) chickpeas (garbanzo beans), drained
⅓ cup Kalamata olives, pitted and chopped
1 yellow or orange bell pepper, chopped
1 red bell pepper, chopped
½ cup red onion, chopped
2 or 3 T fresh parsley, chopped
½ t each salt and black pepper
½ t each dried oregano and basil
½ cup fresh lime or lemon juice
¼ cup sun–dried tomatoes, chopped
1 T olive oil (optional)

At home:
Toss all ingredients together (except for the tomatoes and oil) and, if you have the time, marinate for 4 to 8 hours or overnight. If needed, bring bean mixture to room temperature. Spread on dehydrator silicone mesh sheets. Dry at 135° for about 12 hours. What started out as 7+ cups of bean salad, will eventually dehydrate down to about 2 cups. Cool, add the sun–dried tomatoes, and seal in a baggie. Store in the refrigerator or freezer until ready to use.

On the trail:
Chickpeas take longer to rehydrate, so you need to plan ahead. If having for lunch, right after breakfast fill the baggie with water to the top of the dry bean salad (not to the top of the baggie!) Place in a Nalgene or other plastic container with a tight–fitting screw lid. Store in your pack until ready to eat. The beans should be fully rehydrated in about 4 hours. You can also heat to speed rehydration. Toss with olive if desired.

Asian Somen Salad

This can be a rather bulky lunch to carry, but it's worth the effort.
4 to 6 servings

You'll need:
Pasta:
1 pound somen, udon or angel hair pasta
½ cup soy sauce or tamari
1 t canola oil
1 t Tabasco or other hot sauce

Salad:
2 (10-ounce) cans chicken (optional)
2 cups carrots, slivered
1 can baby corn, chopped
1 cup frozen peas
2 T toasted sesame seeds
2 T toasted sesame oil
1 bunch green onions and tops, sliced
1 can bamboo shoots, chopped
1 can water chestnuts, chopped
2 bell peppers, any colors, chopped

At home:

Pasta: Cook pasta until al dente. Drain. In a large bowl, whisk next 3 ingredients. Toss in warm pasta. Mix well. Spread pasta on fine mesh dehydrator trays. Dry at 135° (about 5 hours). Break into 1–inch pieces.

Salad: Mix all ingredients (except sesame seeds and oil), making sure chicken is shredded. Distribute on fine mesh trays and dehydrate at 160° until thoroughly dried (about 6–7 hours). Then mix the pasta pieces, dried salad and sesame seeds all together. Divide into serving sizes and place in baggies or containers. Package toasted sesame oil in a leak–proof plastic bottle.

On the trail:
About 4 hours before you want to eat, mix equal parts water with dry salad. At lunch drizzle with toasted sesame oil *(don't forget that step!)* Mix well. Let set for a few minutes. This is also good eaten warm.

Carrot–Pineapple Salad

A refreshing alternative to dried foods.
4 servings

You'll need:
1 large lemon, grated and juiced
⅓ cup sugar or ¼ c honey
4 or 5 large carrots
¾ cup crushed pineapple, drained
Optional: slivered almonds, raisins, mayo packets

At home:
Place the grated lemon, juice and sugar in a small pan. Heat slowly until sugar is dissolved. Grate carrots into large bowl. Add pineapple and lemon juice mixture. Toss well. Store in refrigerator for 24 hours to marry flavors. Dehydrate at 135°. Divide portions into baggies.

On the trail:
Add water to the baggie, in equal proportion to the carrot mixture. Leave for 30 minutes to fully rehydrate. Add mix-ins as desired. The mayo will make for a creamier salad.

Napa Slaw

The baggie pictured is the entire contents of this recipe—it really dehydrates down.
6 servings

You'll need:

3 T vinegar (rice, white or any other)
1 T sugar or honey
1 T vegetable oil
3 T soy sauce
1 large Chinese cabbage (napa), sliced
1 bunch scallions, sliced, greens and all
Sesame seeds and toasted slivered almonds

At home:

Mix the vinegar, sugar, oil and soy sauce until sugar is dissolved. Place the cabbage and onions in a large bowl; pour dressing over top and toss well. Marinate in refrigerator for 24 hours. Drain in colander. Spread on fine mesh trays and dehydrate at 135° until dry; portion into baggies. Pack the sesame seeds and almonds separately.

On the trail:

Add water to the baggie to moisten everything well. Let rehydrate for 30 minutes or longer. Sprinkle sesame seeds and almonds over top.

Waldorf Salad

Fashioned after the apple and walnut salad created at the renowned Waldorf Astoria Hotel in New York City, circa late 1800s.
2 servings

You'll need:
2 cups chopped apples, lightly tossed in lemon juice
OR 2 cups freeze–dried apples
½ cup celery, finely diced
½ cup walnuts (or pecans), chopped
2 to 4 single–serving mayonnaise packets
True Lemon or Real Lemon packets (optional)

At home:
Mix the apple and celery. Dehydrate on the fine mesh tray at 135° until completely dry. Allow to cool, then place in a baggie. Place walnuts in a second baggie. Note: If using freeze–dried diced apples,simply dehydrate the celery.

On the trail:
Add just enough water to the apple and celery bag to cover. Rehydrate for at least 3 to 4 hours. If using freeze–dried apples, add a small amount of water to the baggie—the apples almost rehydrate instantaneously. Drain (if needed); add nuts and mayonnaise. If you like a tangy version, add the lemon.

Gingered Apple–Zucchini Salad

The ginger and lemon notes combine to make a light, refreshing salad.
2 servings

You'll need:
1 large apple and 1 large zucchini
¼ c freshly–squeezed lemon juice
1 T sugar or ½ T honey
1 T fresh grated ginger or 1 t ginger powder

At home:
Grate the apple and zucchini into a large bowl. Mix lemon juice, sugar and ginger in another bowl. Combine everything together and toss well. Marinate in refrigerator for several hours or overnight, to marry the flavors. Dehydrate at 135° until dry; portion into baggies as needed.

On the trail: Add a small amount of water to the baggie to moisten everything well. This salad only needs a few minutes to rehydrate, so you can easily add more water if needed. The tangy flavors are refreshing on a hot summer day.

Wakame Seaweed Salad

Use wakame or any seaweed(s) you prefer.
4 servings

You'll need:
1.7 ounces dried wakame seaweed
Dressing:
- 1 T rice vinegar
- 3 T low–sodium soy sauce
- 1 T toasted sesame oil
- 1 T mirin
- 1 t sugar or other sweetener
- ¼ t crushed red pepper
- ½ t ginger powder
- ¼ t garlic powder
- ¼ t onion powder
- 1 T toasted sesame seeds

At home:
If needed, cut the seaweed into narrow strips; place in a baggie. Mix the dressing ingredients and store in a leak–proof bottle. If you plan on using the dressing soon, you can use fresh ginger, garlic and onion. Refrigerate if necessary.

On the trail:
Sprinkle the seaweed with about ½ cup water and let sit for 5 to 10 minutes. Mix seaweed with dressing and sesame seeds; toss well.

Miso Veggie Salad

You can also substitute ⅓ cup of store–bought or any other homemade dressing.
2 servings

You'll need:
2 large carrots (about 1 pound), grated
1 red pepper, diced
¾ cup red onion, diced
¼ to ½ cup greens (cilantro, parsley, baby kale etc), chopped
Dressing: 2 T miso (white or yellow)
1 T seasoned rice vinegar
1 T mirin
2 T toasted sesame oil
1 t fresh grated ginger or ¼ t ginger powder
1 small clove of garlic, minced or ¼ t garlic powder
2 T toasted sesame seeds
½ cup slivered almond (cashews or chow mien noodles can also be used)

At home:
Grate the carrots into a large bowl. Add the peppers, onions, and greens. Toss well. Dehydrate at 135° until dry; portion into baggies as needed. Whisk the dressing ingredients together and store in a leak–proof bottle. If you plan on using the dressing soon, you can use fresh ginger and garlic. Refrigerate if necessary.

On the trail: Add about ½ cup of water to the baggie to moisten everything well. This salad only needs about 15 minutes to rehydrate, so you can easily add more water if needed. You want the salad on the drier and crunchier side, and not mushy. Toss with the dressing, sesame seeds, and almonds.

Southwest Bean Salad

This is good as a stand–alone salad, inside breakfast burritos, or as enchilada filling.
2 servings or more as garnish

You'll need:
1 T vinegar
½ t salt
1 T cilantro (optional)
1 (15.5–ounce) can of kidney beans, drained
1 cup corn (frozen, canned or fresh)
½ poblano or bell pepper (any color), diced
1 or 2 canned chipotle peppers, in sauce
2 green onions, sliced
½ t ground cumin
⅛ t cayenne (to taste)

At home:
Mix the vinegar, salt and cilantro in a large bowl. Add all other ingredients, mixing well. Taste for proper seasoning and adjust if necessary. Marinate in refrigerator for 24 hours, to marry flavors. Dehydrate on either the fine mesh or the fruit–leather tray at 135° until completely dry (about 5 hours). Cool and store in a baggie.

On the trail:
Add water to the baggie in 1:1 ratio (eg., 1 cup water to 1 cup salad). Let rehydrate for 60 minutes or longer. While waiting, go explore the beauty and wonders of a never–ending slot canyon.

This is a great filling to use with the chicken enchiladas recipe on page 113.

Wild Rice Salad with Apples and Pecans

Using a parboiled rice mixture greatly reduces rehydration time.
2 large or 4 small servings

You'll need:
1 cup wild rice mixture*
⅓ cup fresh parsley, chopped
1 large apple, diced
3 green onions, thinly sliced
1 orange, zested and juiced

Dressing:
2 T olive oil
2 T apple cider vinegar
2 t sugar or honey
½ t dry mustard
½ t salt
¼ t freshly ground black pepper

Mix-ins:
¾ cup chopped pecans, ¾ cup dried cranberries (optional)

* Wild rice is wonderful, but it's also rather expensive and takes a long time to cook *and* to rehydrate. A compromise is a parboiled rice mixture, consisting of white, brown, red, and wild rice (there are a couple of variations out on the market), which takes only 15 minutes to cook and is much quicker to rehydrate. It has a similar nutty taste to wild rice.

At home:
Cook the rice per instructions. Chop or dice the parsley, apple, and green onions. Once the rice is cooked, toss with the freshly chopped items, orange juice, and zest. Dehydrate on fine mesh trays at 135° until completely dry. Allow to cool before storing. Mix the dressing ingredients and store in a small leak–proof bottle. Bag the pecans and cranberries separately.

On the trail:
About 3 to 4 hours before you want to eat, mix dry salad with equal parts water. When fully rehydrated, add the pecans and cranberries (if using), and toss with the dressing. You can also eat this warm or hot.

Chicken Curry Salad

There are many different versions of this salad—and they're all good!
4 to 6 servings

You'll need:
Salad:
5 cups *cooked* rice (brown or white)
½ cup rice or white vinegar
4 (10–ounce) cans chicken, well–drained
1 cup diced celery
1 cup diced carrots
1½ cups diced apples
½ cup chopped parsley
1 cup diced red pepper
½ cup diced red onion

Dressing:
⅓ cup olive oil
⅓ cup canola oil
1 T honey
¾ t salt
1½ t garlic powder
1½ t ground cumin
1½ T curry powder

At home:
In a large bowl, mix the warm rice and vinegar. Set aside to cool. Then add all the other salad ingredients. Mix well, making sure the chicken is shredded. Dehydrate at 160° until completely dry (about 5 hours). Divide into serving sizes and place in a large baggie/container. Mix dressing ingredients; store in a leak–proof container.

On the trail:
About 4 hours before you want to eat, mix dry salad with equal parts water. When fully rehydrated, drizzle with dressing (be sure to shake well before using.) Mix everything well. Let sit for a few minutes. Carrots and celery will be crunchy, but apples should be soft.

Tasty Lunch Hacks

Some backpackers like to have a leisurely mid–day meal, while others like to just graze as they hike along. Or maybe an early afternoon shower has discouraged a hot meal. In that case, it's nice to have a few quick and easy lunches packed away for that much–needed energy boost to get you through the day.

- Rehydrated peanut butter powder smeared on tortillas.
- Dry sausages, hard cheeses, olives, and hot–pickled (spicy) vegetables.
- Box of tabbouleh salad mix, garnished with olive oil and a lemon juice packet, served with pita bread.
- Tuna pouches with mayo, mustard, and pickle relish packets + crackers.
- Cans of sardines, smoked oysters, pickled herring, sprats etc.
- Bagel with shelf–stable cream cheese and smoked salmon, topped with thinly–sliced shallot and capers.
- Dried hummus mix (rehydrated), Real Lemon packet, crackers and baby carrots.
- Cinnamon raisin bagel with chocolate hazelnut spread (eg., Nutella)

Sides and Small Plates

There are people who so arrange their lives that they feed themselves only on side dishes.

– Jose Ortega y Gasset

Guacamole

Guacamole makes a great topping for many dishes, as a dip at lunch, or for a dinner appetizer. Use your favorite recipe or the one below. Or take the easy way out!

Home–made Guacamole:

3 avocados, mashed
2 large lemons or 3 limes, juiced
2 Roma tomatoes, diced
3 T diced onion
1 large clove fresh garlic, minced
Dash of hot sauce to taste
½ t sea salt
3 T cilantro, chopped (optional)

At home:

Whoa! That's a lotta' juice! Yes, but to keep the guacamole from turning brown while dehydrating, the acidity of the lemons and limes keeps the avocados that nice bright green color. And if your avocados aren't quite soft to the touch, microwave them for about 30 seconds. For the lemons and limes—roll them firmly on the counter, under your palm, to loosen the membranes and get the juices flowing. Mix everything together, seasoning to taste.

Store–bought Guacamole:

Short on time? Pick up a container of pre–made guac and dehydrate the same way.

To Dehydrate: Spread on a fruit roll sheet and dehydrate at 135⁰ for at least 12 hours. Avocado has lots of that 'good' fat and takes a long time to dehydrate. When it's half–dry, you can gently poke it all over with a fork or turn it over to help release more moisture. Once dry, label and store in the refrigerator or freezer.

On the trail:

Add water to fully saturate the guacamole. Massage baggie, slowly adding more water as needed. If you like your guacamole creamier, you can add single–serving packets of mayonnaise on the trail.

Hummus

You can buy hummus already made in the deli section and dehydrate that directly. Or make your own and then dehydrate it yourself. (Yes, they have instant mixes, too!)

Home–made Hummus:

1 (14–ounce) can chickpeas (garbanzo beans), undrained
¼ cup tahini (toasted sesame paste)
2 T chopped fresh parsley
⅓ cup lemon juice
¼ t ground red pepper
1 T soy sauce or tamari
True Lemon (dry or liquid) packets (optional)
1 clove garlic
1½ t ground cumin
2 T chopped onion
⅛ t finely ground sea salt

At home:
Place all (except lemon packets) in food processor and blend until smooth. You may need to add a bit of water to get the right consistency.

Store–bought Hummus:

The quality of store–bought hummus keeps getting better. Roasted red pepper. Spinach and artichoke. Pine nut. Dark chocolate dessert hummus. Need we say more?

To Dehydrate: Spread the hummus on a fruit roll sheet and dehydrate at 135⁰ for 8 to 12 hours. As it dries, gently prick it all over with a fork, and even turn chunks over, to enhance the drying process. Once crumbly, cool, label and store in the refrigerator or freezer, ready to be used as needed.

On the trail:
Add water to fully saturate the hummus. Massage the baggie, slowly adding more water as needed. Top with extra lemon as desired. Serve with carrots, pita rounds, and/or crackers.

Baba Ganoush

After rehydrating, cut off the tip of the baggie and squeeze out as needed.

Home–made Baba Ganoush:

1 medium eggplant (about 1 pound)
1 large clove garlic, minced
½ of a large lemon, juiced
⅓ cup tahini (toasted sesame paste)
⅛ t coriander or cumin
1 T olive oil
½ t sea salt
Dash of liquid smoke and/or
1 canned chipotle pepper in adobo sauce

At home:

Slice the eggplant length–wise and place cut side down on a cookie sheet (atop a silicone sheet, parchment paper, or lightly brush the cut face of the eggplant with olive oil.) Bake at 450⁰ until the eggplant is completely soft (about 40 minutes). Once cool, use a spoon to scoop the eggplant from the skin and place the pulp in a food processor with all the other ingredients. Blend and adjust seasoning if necessary.

Store–bought Baba Ganoush:

Once again, there's no shame in taking the easy way out.

To Dehydrate: Spread the eggplant mixture on a fruit roll sheet and dehydrate at 135⁰ for 8 to 12 hours. As it dries, gently prick it all over with a fork, and even turn chunks over, to enhance the drying process. Once crumbly, cool, label and store in the refrigerator or freezer, ready to be used as needed.

On the trail:

Add water to fully saturate the baba ganoush. Massage the baggie, slowly adding more water as needed. Serve with carrots, pita rounds, or crackers.

Salsa Roja

Simply buy a jar or make your own favorite home–made salsa, and then dehydrate.

You'll need:

1 jar store–bought salsa or....

- 4 ripe tomatoes (about 1¼ pounds), roughly chopped
- ½ cup red onion, roughly chopped
- 1 large clove of garlic, chopped
- 3 jalapenos, seeded and chopped (or serranos for more heat)
- Small handful of fresh cilantro, roughly chopped (optional)
- Juice and zest of one large lime (a microplane makes zesting easy)
- 2 t ground cumin
- ½ t chili powder
- Salt and freshly ground pepper, to taste
- 1 (15–ounce) can crushed San Marzano tomatoes
- 1 (4.5–ounce) can diced green chiles (mild, medium, or hot)

At home:

Mix everything together, except the Marzano tomatoes and green chiles. Throw into a food processor and grind until you have the desired consistency. Alternately, you can dice everything and then toss for a chunkier salsa—no food processor needed. Add the canned tomatoes and chiles. Mix well. Taste and correct for seasoning.

Evenly spread on a fruit roll sheet (if juicy) or fine mesh screen (if chunky). Dehydrate at 135⁰ until almost dry and leathery (about 4 or 5 hours). Cool and place needed amounts in baggies.

On the trail:

Add water to the baggie to barely cover the salsa. Add more water if needed. This salsa rehydrates quickly and the lime juice helps keep the colors bright.

Salsa Verde

Lightly roasting the tomatillos is the secret to unlocking their light, citrusy flavors. If time is short, you can also just buy a jar of salsa verde and dehydrate that directly.

You'll need:

1 jar store–bought salsa or....

1½ pounds tomatillos
½ medium white or yellow onion, coarsely chopped
2 jalapeno or serrano peppers, chopped
2 gloves garlic, coarsely chopped
¼ t ground cumin
⅛ t salt (to taste)
1 t sugar (optional, but contributes to flavor depth)
½ lime, juiced and zested (use a microplane)
Cilantro to taste

At home:

Cover a cookie sheet with foil, parchment paper, or a silicone baking sheet. Remove the husks from the tomatillos and rinse thoroughly. Roast the tomatillos by cutting in half and placing each one skin side up on the sheet. Broil at 400⁰ for 5 to 7 minutes, until the skins lightly brown. Alternately, you can pan sauté the tomatillos whole, turning them as they lightly brown on each side. Once tomatillos are browned, cool and coarsely chop (leave the skin on the tomatillos). Note: You can also roast or pan sauté the peppers the same way as the tomatillos. A slight carmelization of the pepper skin brings out their flavors as well.

Add all the ingredients to a blender or food processor and grind to a coarse texture. It's best to pulse the salsa to get an even grinding, but you don't want the salsa too soupy. Dehydrate the salsa on fruit leather roll trays at 135⁰ until leathery (about 4 or 5 hours). This recipe makes a full quart of salsa, so you might not want to bring it all on the trail at one time. Cool, crumble, and place needed amounts in baggies.

On the trail:

Add enough water to the baggie to barely cover the salsa, adding more water if needed. Salsa Verde rehydrates quickly and easily.

Mango Salsa

Good on breakfast burritos, a side for lunch, or spread atop dinner enchiladas.

You'll need:
3 large mangoes, any variety, diced
1 red bell pepper, diced
½ cup diced red onion
1 jalapeno, diced (deseeded for less heat)
2 green onions, greens included, sliced
½ cup chopped cilantro (optional)
1 large lime, zested and juiced
⅛ t salt

At home:
Select mangoes that are ripe, but still firm to the touch. No worries if you don't have all the other ingredients in the exact proportions—go by taste and visual appeal. However, your diced pieces should all be about the same size to ensure uniform dehydration times. And a microplane makes zesting a breeze.

Mix everything together and then dehydrate on a fine mesh screen at 135⁰ until almost dry and leathery (about 5 or 6 hours). Cool and place needed amounts in baggies.

The dehydrated salsa on the left is approximately one–half of this recipe or 1½ cups of light–weight bliss. You might be tempted to only dehydrate half and devour the other half fresh before it even hits the dehydrator! Fresh mango, treated with lime juice, dehydrates beautifully and is great as a dried fruit out on the trail.

On the trail:
Add enough water to the baggie to barely cover the salsa, adding more water if needed. Mango salsa rehydrates rather quickly (in about 20 to 30 minutes) and the lime juice helps keep the colors bright.

Refried Beans

Easy to make. Easy to buy. Easy to use. You can also buy 'instant' refried beans.

Home–made Refried Beans:

2 (16–ounce) cans pinto or black beans, drained (about 3 cups)
2 cloves garlic, chopped
½ onion, chopped
½ t cumin
½ t chili powder
½ t sea salt
1 lime, juiced and zested
Chopped cilantro (optional)
Dash of hot sauce, chopped jalapenos or chipotle pepper in adobo sauce (optional)

At home:
Place all the ingredients in a food processor. Lightly blend, leaving it a bit chunky. Adjust seasoning if necessary. You can also use a potato masher.

Canned Refried Beans:

Pick up a can or two of your favorite brand and dehydrate as described below. Or simply buy instant refried beans and miss all the fun of making your own.

To Dehydrate: Spread the bean mixture on a fruit roll sheet and dehydrate at 135⁰ for 4 to 6 hours. Half–way through the drying process, gently prick it all over with a fork, and even turn chunks over, to enhance the drying process. Once crumbly, cool, label and store in the refrigerator or freezer, ready to be used as needed.

On the trail:
Add water to fully saturate the refried beans. Massage baggie, slowly adding more water as needed. These things rehydrate almost immediately!

Spaghetti or Pizza Sauce

Perfect for pastas, pizzas or used in other recipes.

How do I make dehydrated spaghetti sauce? Some of these recipes (eg., Spicy Sausage Scramble) require dehydrated spaghetti sauce powder (even if you're not having spaghetti!) Making dehydrated sauce is really easy, but there are a few tricks. You can use either store–bought or home–made pasta sauce.

First, *lightly* wipe the silicone fruit roll sheet(s) of your dehydrator with vegetable oil. Spread your favorite sauce (the thicker the better) evenly over the tray. Dehydrate at 135° until it cracks on top. You don't want any gooey spots. Once dry, gently peel the leather from the sheet—if the sauce is completely dry, it should come off fairly easily. This 24–ounce jar of sauce dehydrated down to only 5.1 ounces.

Now this is the important part: Take that leather roll–up and place in the freezer for an hour or two. Remove from the freezer, tear into pieces, and then use a mini food processor to grind the leather into a coarse powder. You'll end up with about a cup of powder that will quickly rehydrate! Store in the freezer or refrigerator and use as needed.

On the trail:
Simply add small amounts of water to the spaghetti sauce powder. It usually rehydrates in about 10 minutes. Continue adding water until it is the consistency you are looking for.

Gravies

Good on biscuits, mashed potatoes, stuffing mix and more.

Instant Gravy Package:

There are many instant gravies on the market, including some with questionable ingredients. Typically you just add a cup of water, stir, and heat until thickened.

Homemade Gravy:

3 T beef or chicken bouillon granules
¾ cup all–purpose flour
½ t freshly ground black pepper
1.5 T ghee

Mix all the dry ingredients together. *You only need 2T of this mix to make a small batch of gravy.* Package the ghee separately. At camp, heat the ghee in a small pot or skillet. Stir in 2 T of the gravy mix. Cook for 1 minute. Add ¾ cup water. Bring to a boil; turn down the heat and simmer for 5 minutes, until gravy is thickened.

Vegan Gravy:

2 t vegetable bouillon granules or cubes
¼ cup all–purpose or brown rice flour
3 T nutritional yeast
¾ t onion powder
½ t ground mustard
2 packets soy sauce

Mix all the dry ingredients together. Package the soy sauce separately. At camp, empty the dry mix and the soy sauce into a small pot or skillet. Add 2 cups water. Cook over medium–high heat for a few minutes, until gravy is thickened.

Spicy Cashew Queso

Yummy on burritos, tacos and chips. You may want to double the recipe.

You'll need:
1 cup cashews (roasted, with sea salt)
1 (4–ounce) can diced green chiles
2 chipotle peppers, canned in adobo sauce
2 T nutritional yeast
¼ t fine sea salt

At home:
Place everything in a small food processor, along with a scant ½ cup water. Blend until smooth. Place on a fruit roll sheet and dehydrate at 135° until dry (about 12 hours). Cashews have a lot of natural oil and take time to dehydrate.

Remove from the tray and grind again in the food processor. This will help decrease your rehydration time and give you a nice, smooth sauce. Store in an air-tight container, or freezer, until needed.

On the trail:
Add equal amounts of water to the finely ground queso mix to make a thick dip. For example, add ½ cup water to ½ cup queso mix. Add more water if you want a thinner cheese sauce, for example to spread over burritos or enchiladas.

Heat over a low flame. Allow to sit for about 10 minutes and then heat again, if needed. This seems to thicken the sauce and pull the individual components back together into a full–flavored queso.

Cheese Sauce

Three options here: real cheese; freeze–dried shredded cheese; or powdered cheese. Semi–hard cheeses will keep for several days in the backcountry. You can also add onion or garlic powder, pepper or cayenne to your sauces.

Real Cheese Sauce:

2 T ghee
2 T all-purpose flour (or gluten–free baking mix)
4 T full cream milk powder (NIDO)
8 ounces semi–hard cheese such as cheddar, Gouda, or Gruyere

Package each ingredient separately. At camp, melt the ghee in a small skillet or pot over a medium–low heat. Slowly mix in the flour; stirring constantly, toast for one minute. Add 1 cup water to the milk powder; add to the pan and stir well. Shave the cheese with your pocket knife and add to the same pan. Stir until melted and blended. Best eaten before it sets up.

Freeze-dried Cheese Sauce:

Follow the same directions as above, except substitute 1¾ cups of freeze-dried shredded cheddar cheese for the semi–hard cheese. On the trail, rehydrate the freeze-dried cheese with equal amounts of water for about 10 minutes. Drain and then use as instructed above. Heads up: Freeze-dried cheese never truly 'melts'.

Powdered Cheese Sauce:

⅓ cup high–quality cheddar cheese powder
3 T full cream milk powder (NIDO)
3 T all-purpose flour (or gluten–free baking mix)
3 T ghee

Package the cheese, NIDO and flour together. Store the ghee in a leak–proof container. At camp, heat the ghee, plus 1½ cups water, in a small pot or skillet until simmering. Slowly stir in the dry ingredients, mixing well as you go. Cook over medium–low heat, stirring gently but continuously, until the sauce has thickened.

Tofu Jerky

You can dry tofu jerky in a dehydrator or in the oven.

You'll need:

1 (14–ounce) package of extra–firm tofu
¼ cup soy sauce or tamari
¼ cup Worcestershire sauce
2 T brown sugar, maple syrup or other sweetener
1 t Liquid Smoke
1 t sriracha or other hot sauce (to taste)
¼ t garlic powder
¼ t onion powder

At home:

Drain the tofu and weight with a heavy object (such as an iron skillet or Dutch oven) to press out any extra moisture. Slice the tofu into ⅜" slabs.

Mix all the other ingredients together and place in a non–reactive container (such as metal or ceramic). Add the tofu slabs and marinate at least an hour or up to overnight.

Remove the tofu from the marinade. Place on fine mesh dehydrator sheets and dehydrate at 135° until dry, but still flexible.

Alternately, arrange the tofu slabs on a metal cooling rack (or a silicone baking sheet or parchment paper), set on top of a rimmed cookie sheet. Dry in an oven, set at 200° F. Flip occasionally to ensure even drying. Cool and store in the refrigerator until needed.

Salmon Jerky

Good made with trout, too.

You'll need:
2 lb salmon fillets (skin on), preferably wild caught sockeye salmon
½ cup soy sauce or tamari
¼ cup Worcestershire sauce
3 to 4 t Liquid Smoke
2 T lemon juice
2 T brown sugar
1 t black pepper
1 t crushed red pepper
1 t garlic powder

At home:
Rinse fillets, checking to be sure no bones are remaining. Keep the skin intact, as it helps to hold the jerky together. Pat with paper towel and place in the freezer for an hour or so (to firm the fish and make for easier slicing). Mix the remaining ingredients to make the marinade. Remove the salmon from the freezer and cut crosswise into uniform slabs ¼ to ½ of an inch thick. Place salmon in marinade (in either a large plastic baggie or a nonreactive bowl), cover, and refrigerate for up to 12 hours.

After marinating, drain the salmon and place on dehydrator trays, with lots of air circulation between fillets. Dehydrate at 160° until dry, but still flexible. This will take about 9 to 12 hours, depending on the thickness of your slices. Alternately, a smoker or a oven set on low can be used to dry the fish. Store the jerky in an air–tight container (or vacuum–sealed package) in a cool, dark place for 2 to 3 months. Jerky can also be frozen to extend its shelf–life.

Pesto

Great on pasta, pizza, scrambled eggs and much, much more.

You'll need:

Instant Pesto:

1 package instant pesto mix
Olive oil, as specified on the package (usually 3 T)

Package the recommended amount of oil in a leak–proof bottle. At camp, simply follow the instructions on the package. Typically it's ½ cup water, plus the oil and the mix, heated in a small pan for approximately one minute.

Homemade Pesto: Follow this or your favorite recipe

2 cups fresh greens, tightly packed (basil, spinach, kale, stinging nettle, etc)
½ t sea salt
2 cloves fresh garlic, minced
⅓ c ground nuts (pine nuts, almonds, walnuts, etc)
½ c dried grated cheese (Parmesan, Romano, etc)
½ c extra virgin olive oil

Place the greens, salt and garlic in a small food processor and grind until the desired consistency. You may need to add a little bit of water to get the greens to process. Do not add the oil. To dehydrate, smear the greens onto a fruit roll–up sheet and dehydrate at 135° until dry. Cool, then store in a baggie.

Package the nuts, dried Parmesan cheese, and olive oil separately. The latter should be in a leak–proof container.

On the trail:

Rehydrate pesto with just a little bit of water. It should rehydrate rather quickly. Mix in the ground nuts, Parmesan, and olive oil. Stir until you have a nice, smooth consistency.

Keep in mind that a little pesto goes a long way. For example, 2 large tablespoons of pesto is enough to cover a medium-sized pizza or coat a pound of pasta. Unless you're like Elijah, who can eat it by the spoonful.

Kimchi

A traditional Korean dish made of fermented vegetables.

You'll need:
1 jar of store–bought kimchi (dehydrate as described below)

Or make your own, such as
Veggies: 2 pounds napa cabbage, cut into strips or chunks
2 cups daikon radish or carrot, cut into matchsticks
2 bunches green onions, chopped (greens and all)
¼ cup sea salt

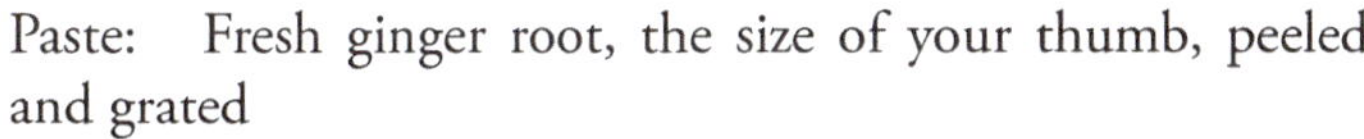

Paste: Fresh ginger root, the size of your thumb, peeled and grated
4 large or 6 small cloves garlic, peeled and minced
4 T Korean–style red pepper flakes or chili garlic sauce
2 T fish sauce or soy sauce
2 t sugar, honey or other sweetener (optional)
3 T miso paste (optional)

At home:
Place the cabbage in a large bowl and toss with the salt. Add just enough water to cover the cabbage; use a plate (with added weight if necessary) to keep everything submerged. Let sit at room temperature for 6 to 8 hours. Drain well, but reserve the brine. Add the radish, carrots and green onions. Mix well.

Grind the paste ingredients in a small food processor until thick. Massage the veggies with the paste, until everything is thoroughly coated.

Lightly pack into two 1–quart jars, leaving about 1 to 2 inches of headroom. Add some of the leftover brine to full submerge the veggies. Loosely cover and store in a cool, dark place for 72 hours. If you've not made kimchi before, it would be good to google this part of the process—it's easy, but there are a few nuances you might want to know. Once fermented, drain well and dehydrate.

To Dehydrate:
Dry on fine mesh screens at 135⁰ for 4 hours or so. *You may want to dehydrate this outside, after giving your neighbors ample warning.* Cool, then pack in an air–tight container until needed.

On the trail:
Add just enough water to the baggie of dehydrated kimchi to cover the veggies. The kimchi will rehydrate quickly. You can also add a tuna packet and call it lunch.

BrocCauli Bake

Easy to put together and best eaten warm right out of the cup.
4 servings

You'll need:
½ cup freeze–dried broccoli
½ cup freeze–dried cauliflower
½ cup couscous
¼ cup OvaEasy egg crystals
1 t powdered chicken or vegetable bouillon
¼ t onion powder
2 cheese sticks or their equivalent

At home:
Package all the dry ingredients into one baggie. Throw in two cheese sticks.

On the trail:
Add 2 cups of water to the baggie of dry ingredients; mix well. Evenly distribute the batter amongst 4 silicone baking cups—make sure the couscous and veggie proportions are the same in each cup, as the couscous tends to sink to the bottom and the veggies float to the top.

Using the hot–water bath cooking instructions on page 10, cook at a low boil for about 12 to 15 minutes. You'll see tiny cracks just starting to form on the surface of each 'muffin' as the egg sets up. Top with whittled cheese. That's it!

(You can also cook this right in your pot, but be careful because egg tends to really stick to things and make clean–up more difficult.)

Artichoke and Sweet Pepper Fritters

Try not to omit the balsamic—it really brightens this dish.
2 large servings

You'll need:
1 (14–ounce or so) can of artichoke quarters (in brine, not oil)
1 large sweet bell pepper, sliced or chopped (about ½ cup dehydrated peppers)
¾ cup all–purpose flour or gluten–free baking mix
4 T full cream milk powder (NIDO)
4 T OvaEasy whole egg crystals
½ t baking powder
½ t garlic powder
¼ t onion powder
½ t salt
¼ t black pepper
dash cayenne
3 packets True Lemon
Oil or ghee
Balsamic glaze or reduction

At home:
Place the artichoke quarters and sweet pepper on a fine mesh screen and dehydrate at 135⁰ until leathery. Package the artichokes and peppers in one baggie. Package the dry ingredients in another baggie. Package separately the oil or ghee and balsamic in leak–proof bottles.

On the trail:
Add 1 cup of water to the baggie of dehydrated artichokes and peppers. They should rehydrate in about 30 minutes. Once rehydrated, add the veggies (water and all) to the bag of dry ingredients and mix well.

Spoon the batter into an oiled pan and saute until brown. Flip and brown again. You may need to flatten the fritter to get the insides to cook properly. Generously drizzle with balsamic glaze or reduction. Serve warm.

Savory Corn Cakes

Try them topped with mango salsa or salsa verde (page 73 – 74).
Makes 8 (3") cakes

You'll need:

½ cup ground cornmeal
½ cup gluten–free baking mix
1 t baking powder
½ t baking soda
½ t salt
¼ t onion powder
¼ t ancho chili powder
½ t ground cumin
4 T NIDO
4 T OvaEasy whole egg crystals
1 cup freeze–dried corn
3 T ghee or oil

At home:
Combine all the dry ingredients into one baggie. Package the ghee or oil in a leak–proof container. Note: You can also substitute regular all-purpose flour for the GF.

On the trail:
Add ½ cup water to the baggie and massage gently, but thoroughly. Let rest for 5 to 10 minutes. You may need to add a bit more water to get a good, thick batter.

Over medium heat, warm the ghee/oil in a pan. Carefully tear off the bottom corner of the baggie (creating about a 1–inch gash), to squeeze the batter into your hot pan. Cook until lightly browned on the bottom. Flip and cook again. Best served warm. Also delicious as a side to hot soups.

Corn Custard

Best eaten warm, right out of the cup.
4 servings

You'll need:
1½ cups freeze–dried corn
6 T full cream milk powder (NIDO)
4 T OvaEasy whole egg crystals
¾ t salt
Pinch of freshly ground black pepper

At home:
Combine all the dry ingredients into one baggie. Pack 4 silicone baking cups. Dehydrated corn can also be used, but be sure to rehydrate it before baking.

On the trail:
Add 1½ cups water to the baggie and massage gently, but thoroughly. Let rest for 5 minutes while you assemble the cookware. Carefully distribute the corn and custard mix into the 4 silicone baking cups.

Using the instructions on page 10, bake the corn custard in a hot water bath for 10 minutes (or less). You don't need a hard boil—a soft boil works just as well and saves fuel. The tops of each custard cup will bounce back when gently pressed with the back of a spoon.

You can see from the photo at the bottom left that the custard will set up on the bottom of the cup and the corn will float to the top. The steam for the hot water bath renders the corn sweet and the custard silky smooth.

Southwest Baked Beans

This easy recipe makes a lot—perfect for eating and then dehydrating any leftovers.

You'll need:

2 cans (15 ounces) dark-red kidney beans
1 can (15 ounces) black beans
1 can (15 ounces) white kidney beans
1 can (28 ounces) Italian plum tomatoes, drained and chopped
1 onion, chopped
2 large cloves of garlic, chopped
¼ cup dark molasses
2 t dried oregano
2 t dried mustard
1½ t ground ginger
¼ cup cider vinegar
2 T honey
1 t chili powder
2 t ground cumin
salt to taste

At Home:

Lightly rinse and drain the beans in a colander. Place in an oven–proof casserole dish or Dutch oven. Add remaining ingredients and mix gently. Bake at 350^0, covered, for 45 minutes. Remove cover; stir and bake, uncovered, for another 30 minutes until hot and bubbly. Dehydrate on a fruit roll tray at 135^0 until dry. Cool and store in baggies.

On the trail:

Add just enough water to cover the beans. To speed up rehydration, cover, heat to a simmer, turn off heat, and let sit until beans are soft. Heat again as needed.

Roasted Veggies

The double–elixir of roasting and then dehydrating your veggies.

You'll need:
Any vegetables you love
Flavorings of choice, including spices, herbs, lemon, balsamic vinegar etc.
Olive or other oil—it only takes a small amount, eg., 1 T per head of cauliflower

Roasted vegetables are a treat out on the trail. Simply roast your favorites and then dehydrate for use as stand–alone sides, burrito and enchilada fillings, omelet ingredients, or to add to soups and stews. Roasting sweetens and intensifies the flavors of the vegetables, while dehydrating further concentrates those flavors while removing even more moisture from the cellular structure. The veggies may not be the prettiest things once dehydrated, but they really pack down nicely.

At Home:
Preheat oven to 425^0 F. If you have a convection oven, adjust accordingly. Wash veggies and cut into uniform sizes and shapes. Toss gently to *lightly* coat in oil. Toss again with flavorings of your choice. Evenly distribute veggies on a large cookie or roasting sheet. Once oven is preheated, roast veggies until they just begin to crisp and caramelize. You may want to shake the pan or toss the veggies a few times to promote even roasting. Then dehydrate at 135^0 until nearly dry and leathery. Cool and bag as needed. For storage beyond a few days (weeks), freezing is best.

On the trail:
Add enough water to the baggie of veggies to cover. Some vegetables dehydrate very quickly (such as onions, mushrooms, and cabbage), while others can take 3 to 4 hours (including carrots, parsnips, and potatoes), depending on size.

Bannock (Scottish Skillet Bread)

Feel free to switch up the grains to your liking.
Makes 2 servings

You'll need:
½ cup all–purpose flour
½ cup whole wheat flour
¼ cup NIDO
2 t baking powder
¼ t salt
2 T ghee
1 T oil

At home:
Combine all the dry ingredients into one baggie. Package the ghee and oil in separate leak–proof containers.

On the trail:
Bring ½ c water to a simmer and add the ghee. Heat until just melted. Add the dry ingredients and mix well until a dough forms. Massage dough in your hands, then form into a ball.

Heat the oil in a pan or pot. Add the dough ball and gently squash flat until it fills the bottom of the cooking vessel. Heat over medium or medium–low heat for about 5 minutes. Flip and heat for another 4 minutes. Note: This bread is difficult to cook over a jet–boil or similar stove in which the heat is extremely concentrated. You may need a diffuser.

Variations: 1) Form into small patties and make biscuit–sized bread; 2) Add herbs of choice (eg. rosemary, thyme, or garlic) to make a savory bread; 3) Add sugar, cinnamon, raisins, nuts etc. to make a sweet bread. Extra ghee slathered on top is always appreciated!

Chapatis

A good accompaniment to many a meal.
Makes 6 (6") chapatis

You'll need:
1cup all–purpose flour
1 cup whole wheat flour
1 t salt
¼ t garlic powder (optional)
2 T oil

At home:
Mix the dry ingredients into one quart–size freezer baggie. Package the oil in a leak–proof container. No additional oil is needed to cook the chapatis.

On the trail:
Slowly add the oil to the baggie of dry ingredients. Mix well. Add ¼ cup water and mix well again. Add an additional ½ cup water, mix again, then knead in the baggie for about 4-5 minutes. This really keeps your hands and pots clean, but you can also do this outside of the baggie. Let the dough rest for 5 to 10 minutes.

Divide the dough into 6 portions. Roll each portion into a ball, then roll flat like you (or someone else) would for a pie crust. Roll from the center and then to the outer edges (not just back and forth over the same area). A Nalgene bottle or Hydro Flask works great as a rolling pin. And these super thin, plastic cutting boards are perfect for a non–stick, working surface.

Heat a skillet or bottom of your camp pot until very hot (a drop of water should dance merrily across it's surface.) Cook the chapati until it starts to brown on one side (about 60 to 90 seconds), flip, cook again. You should start to see the chapati puff up in various places as the hot air gets trapped between the layers of dough. Flip again if needed. Best served warm.

Cornbread

Easy to dress up or down, and cook in a multitude of ways.
Servings: This is enough batter to fill an 8 or 9" baking pan; make 4 to 6 fry cakes; or fill 4 silicone cups baked in a hot water bath.

You'll need:
¾ cup all–purpose flour or gluten–free baking mix
¾ cup corn meal
2 T sugar or other sweetener
3 T full cream milk powder (NIDO)
2 T OvaEasy whole egg crystal
2 t baking powder
½ t baking soda
¾ t salt
3 T oil
Optional dress–ups: dried sweet peppers or jalapenos; freeze–dried corn; ghee; maple syrup; apple butter or jam.

At home:
Combine all the dry ingredients into one baggie. Package the oil in a leak–proof container.

On the trail:
Add about 2 T of oil and ¾ cup water to the baggie of dry ingredients. Massage well. Use the remaining 1 T oil to coat your baking pan or skillet. Cut off the corner of the baggie and squeeze into your baking pan, skillet or silicone cups (as described on pages 10–12).

The cornbread pictured here was baked in the 8" Fry–Bake pan. The stove heat was kept on low for 4 minutes; the upper heat (twig fire) was kept very hot for an additional 3 minutes. As you can see, both heat levels were a bit too hot—otherwise the cornbread was moist and nicely browned. And no complaints!

Corn Tortillas

Yes, you can always pack in store–bought. But camp–made is fun, too.
Makes about 12 (6") tortillas.

You'll need:
2 cups Masa Harina (a soft corn flour made with limewater)
½ t fine sea salt

At home:
Measure the Masa Harina and the salt into a quart–sized freezer baggie.

On the trail:
Add 1½ cups of very warm water to the masa and salt mixture. Massage gently, but thoroughly. If the dough is crumbly, add another tablespoon or so of water. Continue adding a very small amount of warm water to the mix, until a soft dough forms that you can gently knead with your hands.

Divide the dough into small golf–sized balls. Using a water bottle, roll each dough ball into a circle. If the dough is sticking, split the baggie into two sides, place one side on top of and one side under the dough ball, and then roll. You can also use the bottom of two plates or two pans to compress the dough into a circle.

Place a pan or skillet over medium–high heat. Quickly cook each tortilla, flipping once or more often as needed. Usually a minute on each side is sufficient for small brown spots to form on the tortilla, letting you know it is done. Stack the cooked tortillas into a single tower. Best eaten warm.

Dinners and other Feasts

May your trails be crooked, winding, lonesome, dangerous,
leading to the most amazing view.

– Edward Abbey

Chicken and Broccoli with Sun–dried Tomatoes

This dinner is a little bulky, but it has great color and flavor out on the trail!
4 large servings

You'll need:

½ t garlic powder
½ t salt
1 t rosemary
¼ t crushed red pepper
2 cups freeze–dried chicken
1 pound pasta, your choice
½ cup dry grated Parmesan
¼ t onion powder
¼ t ground black pepper
2 t powdered chicken bouillon
½ cup sun–dried tomatoes, julienned
2 cups freeze–dried broccoli florets
2 T ghee or olive oil

At home:

Place the top 10 ingredients into one baggie. Individually package the pasta, ghee or olive oil, and grated Parmesan separately.

On the trail:

In a large pot, boil water for the pasta. When the pasta is almost done, drain off all the water, except for about 1½ cups. (If you forget, simply add another 1½ cups water back to the pot and heat again.) Add the ghee or oil and stir. Slowly add the chicken, broccoli and spice bag to the pot; gently stir and heat again. Turn off heat and let sit for 10 minutes. Add more water if needed to fully rehydrate everything. Serve with Parmesan cheese.

Salmon Orzo in Lemon Garlic Sauce

Orzo is a fun pastina, but feel free to use any kind of pasta. And if you like capers, they really make this dish zing.
4 servings

You'll need:

For the sauce:
- 1 t garlic powder
- ¼ t onion powder
- 1 t dill
- ¼ t ground black pepper
- 1½ t powdered chicken or veggie bouillon
- ¼ t crushed red pepper
- 6 T full cream milk powder (NIDO)
- 6 to 10 packets of True Lemon
- 1½ t cornstarch

For the pasta:
- 1 pound orzo, or pasta of choice
- 1 T ghee or oil
- 1 or 2 (5–ounce) salmon pouches; salmon jerky (page 79); or shelf–stable smoked salmon
- 4 T capers (to taste)

At home:
Measure all sauce ingredients and place in a small baggie. Package the pasta and other ingredients as needed. Jarred capers are both pickled and salted, so they will keep for several days.

On the trail:
In a large pot, boil water for the pasta. When the pasta is almost done, drain off all the water, except for about 1½ cups of liquid. Add the ghee or oil to the pasta and toss to coat. Slowly sprinkle the dry sauce ingredients over the pasta, stirring continually. Gently break the salmon into chunks, add to the pot, and stir again. Heat through and serve adorned with capers.

Smoked Sausage and Cabbage

One of Kathy's favorites.
4 servings

You'll need:
2 large cloves garlic, thinly sliced
1 medium onion, chopped
8 cups coarsely chopped cabbage
1 t sugar (optional, but adds flavor depth)
1 or 2 t caraway seeds
Salt and pepper to taste
1 T canola oil
12 to 14 oz. shelf-stable sausage or salami (eg., summer sausage; soppressata, Calabrese or Genoa salami, etc.)

At home:
Heat a very small amount of oil in a large skillet over medium–high heat. Sauté the garlic, onion and cabbage until slightly browned and caramelized. Add the sugar, caraway seeds, salt, and pepper; mix well. Place the cabbage mixture on fine mesh dehydrator trays. Dehydrate at 135° until dry. Once cool, place in a baggie, and store until ready to use.

On the trail:
Slice the sausage or salami into thin half–moons or small chunks, and heat in a skillet. Meanwhile, add just enough water to the cabbage baggie to barely cover. The cabbage and onion rehydrates quickly. Combine both summer sausage and cabbage in skillet and heat through.

Mushroom Stroganoff

A quick and easy sauce to pour over the carb of your choice.
One large serving

You'll need:
1 cup dried mushrooms (any kind)
2 T full cream milk powder (NIDO)
2 T all–purpose flour
½ t ground thyme
½ t powdered onion
½ t beef or vegetable bouillon granules
⅛ t ground pepper
⅛ t salt
1 T ghee (optional)
Pasta or rice of choice

At home:
You can dehydrate your own mushrooms by simply slicing into even widths, laying on a dehydrator tray, and dehydrating at 135° until dry. Or pick some dried 'shrooms up at your local store. Mix the other dry ingredients into a baggie. Pack ghee and pasta (or rice) separately. Note: Egg noodles are fragile but they cook in 3 minutes.

On the trail:
Add 2 cups of water to a small pot. Add the dried mushrooms and let sit for 10 or 20 minutes. Then add all the other dry ingredients (except for the pasta and rice). Bring to a boil, stirring occasionally. Reduce heat to low and simmer for about 3 or 4 minutes, until thickened. Add ghee, stir gently until melted, to give the sauce a richer finish.

Depending on what type of pasta or rice you're fixing, be sure to get that pot going so you can time everything together. Then pour the mushroom stroganoff over the carb of your choice. This sauce is also tasty over mashed potatoes!

Black Bean Burgers

A healthy, hearty stick–to–your–ribs burger.
2 servings

You'll need:
1 cup dehydrated or freeze–dried black beans
¼ cup panko or other dried bread crumbs
1T OvaEasy whole egg crystal
1 or 2 T dried chopped peppers
1 t onion powder
½ t garlic powder
½ t ground cumin
½ t ground smoked paprika
½ t ground chili powder
⅛ t salt + ⅛ t fresh ground black pepper

Plus:
1 large pita bread pocket or 2 petite pitas
Oil (packed in a small, plastic leak-proof bottle)
Packets of mayo, mustard, ketchup, hot sauce, pickle relish and so forth

At home:
It's easy to make your own dehydrated black beans—simply take canned beans and dehydrate on fine mesh sheets at 135° until dry. Once dry, *coarsely* chop in a mini food processor (or lightly crush with a rolling pin) to speed up the rehydration process. (If using freeze–dried black beans, *coarsely* chop as well.) Other types of beans can also be substituted. (You can also buy dried bean flakes from places such as Frontier Co–op, but the finer texture isn't the same.) Then mix the beans with all the other ingredients in one baggie.

On the trail:
Add ½ cup water to the baggie to make a thick mixture—remember, you can always add more water if it's too thick, but it's hard to remove excess moisture. You want something the consistency, but not taste, of kindergarten Play–Doh. Allow to sit for 30 minutes.

Form bean mixture into patties. You can also use the baggie to help form a 'burger' without getting your hands all mucked up. Heat the oil in your pan over a medium–low flame. Pan fry the burgers until cooked through and the outside is lightly caramelized. Throw pitas on top of warm skillet to heat. Serve burger tucked into pita bread, with condiments of choice.

Salmon Burgers

Watch out—even the grizzlies might go for these!
2 servings

You'll need:
2 (2.5–ounce) pouches of shelf-stable salmon
¼ cup panko or other dried bread crumbs
1T OvaEasy whole egg crystal
½ t dried rosemary
½ t dried dill
1 t dried onion powder
1 t dried parsley
⅛ t salt

Plus:
1 large pita bread pocket or 2 petite pitas
Oil (packed in a small, plastic leak-proof bottle) or ghee
Packets of soy sauce, mayo, mustard, hot sauce, pickle relish of choice

At home:
Place all the dry ingredients in a small baggie (everything except the salmon). Package everything else separately. Note: If using flavored salmon, you may want to adjust or omit the spices and herbs suggested.

On the trail:
Combine the salmon with the dry ingredients. Add ¼ cup water to the baggie. Allow to sit for 15–20 minutes to fully rehydrate.

Form salmon mixture into patties. You can also use the baggie to help form a 'burger' without getting your hands all mucked up. Heat oil in a small skillet over a medium–low flame. Pan fry until lightly crispy on the outside and cooked through.

Throw pitas on top of warm skillet to heat. Pocket the salmon burgers and serve with choice of condiments.

Tuna Burgers

You can tune a piano, but you can't tune a ....
2 servings

You'll need:
2 (2.5–ounce) pouches of shelf-stable tuna
½ cup panko or other dried bread crumbs
1 T OvaEasy whole egg crystal
½ t dried celery
1 t each dried onion powder, mustard powder, dried parsley

Plus:
1 large pita bread pocket or 2 petite pitas
Oil (packed in a small, plastic leak-proof bottle) or ghee
Packets of soy sauce, mayo, mustard, hot sauce, pickle relish of choice

At home:
Place all the dry ingredients in a small baggie (everything except the tuna). Package everything else separately. Note: If using flavored tuna, you may want to adjust or omit the spices and herbs suggested.

On the trail:
Combine the tuna with the dry ingredients. Add ⅓ cup water to the baggie to make a thick mixture. Allow to sit for 15–20 minutes.

Form tuna mixture into patties. You can also use the baggie to help form a 'burger' without getting your hands all mucked up. Heat oil in a small skillet over a medium–low flame. Pan fry until lightly crispy on the outside and cooked through.

Throw pitas on top of warm skillet to heat. Pocket the tuna burgers and serve with choice of condiments.

Mini Mountain Meatloaf

You can bake this using a hot–water bath or just fry patties in a skillet.
2 large servings

You'll need:
1¼ cup dehydrated or freeze–dried hamburger or soysage crumbles
½ cup panko or other dried bread crumbs
2½ T OvaEasy whole egg crystal
¼ cup dried chopped peppers
⅓ cup dehydrated spaghetti sauce powder (page 76)
1 t dried onion powder
1 t dried garlic powder
⅛ t each salt and pepper
Extra packets of ketchup or hot sauce
Silicone bowl to fit your pot, or a small amount of oil

At home:
If dehydrating the meat yourself, cook the beef until done. Drain well and pat with paper towels. Dehydrate on a fine mesh tray at 160° until dry. If using a plant–based product, dehydrate on a fine mesh tray at 130° until dry (pictured above). Once cool, place the hamburger or soysage in a baggie with all the other ingredients (except for the packets of ketchup and oil).

On the trail:
Add two cups of water to the baggie, mix well, and let sit for 20–30 minutes. You want something that looks like raw meatloaf, but not too wet. This recipe makes about 4 cups of 'raw' meatloaf. Using the hot–water bath method on page 10, bake the meatloaf in silicone liners or bowls for about 20 to 25 minutes, until firm on the top. Carefully remove from pot and cool a few minutes before inverting.

You can also shape the raw meatloaf into large patties, pan fry until crispy and lightly caramelized on the outside, and cooked through.

Serve with extra packets of ketchup or hot sauce, if desired.

Spaghetti and Mushroom Balls

Much sought after comfort food, with an oh–so–good twist. These mushroom balls are also great formed into patties and sautéed like burgers.
4 servings

You'll need:
For the balls:
- 1 pound mushrooms, dehydrated (about 3.5 ounces dried)
- ½ cup chopped walnuts or pecans
- ¾ cup panko or other dried bread crumbs
- ¼ cup dry Parmesan cheese
- 2 T OvaEasy whole egg crystal
- 1 T dried onion
- 2 t garlic powder
- 1 T dry parsley
- ½ t dried basil
- ½ t dried oregano
- ½ t salt
- ¼ t red pepper flakes

1 jar pasta sauce, dehydrated (see page 76)
1 pound thin spaghetti or other pasta
Oil packed into a small plastic leak–proof bottle
Extra packets of Parmesan cheese, hot sauce, and so forth

At home:
Slice the mushrooms into even widths (¼ inch or so) and dehydrate at 135° until dry (4 to 5 hours). You can also buy dried mushrooms. After drying, either chop the mushrooms into pea–sized pieces, or simply throw into a mini food processor and let technology work its magic. Then place the dried mushrooms and all the other 'ball' ingredients into one baggie. Package the other items as needed.

On the trail:
Add just enough water to the mushroom bag to *lightly* soak the ingredients (½ to ⅔ cup water or so), and set aside. You want a good thick mixture. Meanwhile, rehydrate the spaghetti sauce the same way and start heating the pasta water.

When everything is rehydrated, start the pasta cooking in one pot. Heat a small amount of oil in a skillet over medium heat. When the oil is hot, use a spoon and scoop small rounded balls of mushroom mixture into the pan; cook until browned on the outside and hot in the inside. When all the mushroom balls are cooked, pour the spaghetti sauce in the skillet and heat all together. Serve over pasta.

Chicken and Dumplings

Gotta' give it to the scouts for this one...
2 servings

You'll need:

Soup:
- 2 t dried onions
- 2 t dried celery
- 1 t dried parsley
- 2 T chicken bouillon or cubes
- 1 cup freeze-dried or 1 pouch chicken
- ¼ t black pepper
- ¼ t salt
- ½ cup instant potatoes
- 2 cups freeze-dried mixed vegetables

Dumplings:
- 2 T full cream milk powder (NIDO)
- ½ cup baking mix (eg., Bisquick)

At home:
Place the soup ingredients into one baggie. (If using a chicken pouch, keep that separate.) Combine the dumpling ingredients in another baggie.

On the trail:
Pour the soup ingredients, along with 4 cups water, into a large pot. Bring to a gentle boil. Meanwhile, add a few tablespoons of water to the dumpling baggie and massage until well mixed (you can always add more water, if needed). Once water boils, reduce heat to simmer. Tear a hole in the corner of the dumpling bag and squeeze dollops onto the top of the simmering soup. Cover pot, try not to peak, and simmer for another 20 minutes.

Beef Filet Mignon

Slowly sip your aperitif of choice, then ask your unsuspecting guests how they like their steaks cooked.

You'll need:
1 filet per person
Sea salt and crushed black pepper
Garlic clove(s)
Fresh rosemary
Ghee

At home:
Buy prepackaged filets or straight from the butcher case. Freeze individual filets and place each in it's own baggie. Plan on cooking the first or second night out.

On the trail:
Frozen filets will last at least 24 hours, so time your dinner accordingly. Heat ghee in bottom of pot or pan until hot. Place filet in pan, add salt and pepper as desired, then sear on both sides until meat is caramelized. This should take about 1-2 minutes per side. Add crushed garlic and rosemary to the pan, swirling until the ghee is saturated with flavor. Spoon melted ghee on top of the filet. Cover with a lid and cook on low heat until the filet is cooked to your liking. This really isn't hard at all and your friends will be SO impressed when it's your night to cook.

Sides:
You may as well go all out. Pack in some fresh veggies found in those cellophane bags at the grocery store. Or bring some freeze-dried asparagus or green beans. Alternately, you can roast veggies at home (simply toss in olive oil, season, and roast in the oven) before dehydrating (see page 89). Don't forget dessert!

Creamy Grits Country–Girl Style

The ghee and soy sauce pairing contributes to the umami flavors of this dish.
Makes 2 servings

You'll need:

For the 'Style':	1.5 ounces dried mushrooms (8 ounces fresh)
	⅔ cup soy crumbles, dehydrated (or 'real' sausage crumbles)
	1 t garlic powder
	1 t thyme
	½ t freshly ground pepper
	1 or 2 T soy sauce (about 2 to 3 packets)
For the Grits:	½ cup 5–minute grits (instant grits work, but aren't quite as good)
	½ cup full cream milk powder (NIDO)
	1 T Parmesan
	⅛ t salt
Ghee:	6 T total

At home:
For the 'Style': Buy dried mushrooms or dehydrate your own. Same for the crumbles. Package all the ingredients in one baggie; package the soy sauce separately.
For the Grits: Package all the ingredients in one baggie.
Ghee: Package as needed.

On the trail:
For the 'Style': Add enough water to the dried mushrooms and crumbles to rehydrate. Heat 4 T ghee in a skillet. Add all the 'style' ingredients and heat thoroughly (including any leftover liquid).

For the Grits: Boil 2 cups of water. Slowly add the grits mixture and remaining 2 T of ghee, stirring as you go. Simmer on low for about 5 minutes. Top with style!

Southern Comfort

This meal easily comes together in less than 15 minutes.
2 servings

You'll need:
6 ounces country ham, vacuum–packed
1 cup freeze–dried green beans
1 cup instant mashed potatoes (any flavor)

At home:
Package the green beans and potatoes in small baggies. Unopened, the country ham will keep indefinitely. "Biscuit–size" ham pieces fit nicely into smaller pans.

On the trail:
Place the country ham in a skillet or the bottom of your cook pot. Cook over medium–low heat; lightly brown on one side. Flip and brown on the other.

Meanwhile add a cup of water to the baggie of green beans. Add another cup of water to the baggie of instant potatoes. Mix well. Both the green beans and the potatoes should be fully rehydrated by the time the ham is done cooking. Push the ham to one side of the pan; scoop the beans into the pan; then squeeze the potatoes into the remaining space. Heat everything thoroughly, being careful not to overcook (thus dry out) the ham. The saltiness of the ham and the potatoes will nicely season the beans.

Creamy Vegan Tofu Pasta

Easy to add roasted veggies or serve as is. Depending on how much sauce you like, this could be enough for 2 pounds pasta.

You'll need:

1 (14–ounce) package firm tofu, reserving liquid
2 cloves garlic, roughly chopped
¼ cup chopped onion or green scallions
½ cup roughly chopped cilantro, parsley or other greens, leaves and fine–stems
2 t toasted sesame oil
1 T chili oil
1 T white or rice vinegar
2 T soy sauce
½ t garam masala or 5–spice powder
1 t ginger powder (or 2 t freshly–grated)
1 t sugar or honey
¼ t sea salt
1 pound pasta
Toasted sesame seeds

At Home:

Place all ingredients, except for the pasta and sesame seeds, in a small food processor. Add the reserved liquid and blend until creamy. If necessary add additional water. Spread over 1 or 2 fruit roll–up trays and dehydrate at 135^{0} until dry and crumbly. Cool and store until needed. Package pasta of choice and sesame seeds for the trail.

On the trail:

Add enough water to the baggie of dehydrated tofu sauce to cover. While it's dehydrating, cook pasta. Drain and add the tofu sauce. Gently mix over low heat. Serve sprinkled with sesame seeds.

African Peanut Stew

The rich flavors of this stew rehydrate beautifully out on the trail.
6 servings

You'll need:

For the spice paste:

- 2 onions, chopped
- 5 cloves garlic, chopped
- 1 t chili powder
- 2 t ground coriander
- 1 t ground turmeric
- 2 t ground cumin
- ½ t ground mustard
- 1 thumb–sized piece of fresh ginger, peeled and diced

For the stew:

- 2 T oil (peanut or other)
- 1 pound sweet potatoes, chopped
- 3 T tomato paste
- 1 (14–ounce) can diced tomatoes (1½ cups)
- 2 (14–ounce) cans black–eye peas or garbanzos (3 cups)
- 3 cups vegetable (or chicken) stock
- ½ cup natural peanut butter
- Salt and freshly ground pepper, to taste
- 16 ounces fresh greens (spinach, kale etc.)
- 2 T lemon juice
- Extra packets of True Lemon or Lime; hot sauce

At home:

Add all the spice paste ingredients to a food grinder or processor; grind into a coarse paste. Heat oil in a large, heavy–bottomed pot over medium–low heat. Add the paste, stirring frequently so it doesn't stick, for 8–10 minutes until lightly browned and aromatic. Add all the other stew ingredients, except for the greens and lemon juice. Cover with a lid and simmer until potatoes are tender (about 20 to 30 minutes). Remove from heat and add greens and lemon juice. Dehydrate stew on fruit roll–up trays at 135° until dry. Cool and store portions in baggies, along with packets.

On the trail:

Add the dehydrated stew to a pot, adding just enough water to cover, and heat gently. Turn off heat and allow to sit for an hour or so. Then cook again to fully rehydrate and heat through. Serve topped with wild onion greens, if available.

Cuban Picadillo

A little spicy,. A little salty. A little sweet. Don't be afraid to try this one. It's a keeper!
Makes 4 large or 6 medium servings

You'll need:

1¼ pounds lean or grass-fed ground beef
1 large onion, chopped
1 large green bell pepper, chopped
2 large cloves garlic, minced
½ cup good, dark beer (or bouillon)
3 T tomato paste
1 (15–ounce) can diced tomatoes with green chiles
2 t ground cumin
1¼ t ground coriander
½ t oregano
1½ t salt
¼ t black pepper
½ t hot sauce (to taste)

2 T cooking oil
1 pound baking potatoes, cut into ½-inch pieces
⅔ cup raisins (or more to taste)
⅔ cup halved and pitted green olives (or more to taste)

Flour or corn tortillas, extra hot sauce packets

At home:

In a large frying pan, cook the ground beef until no longer pink. Add the onion, bell pepper, and garlic. Cook, stirring occasionally, until veggies start to soften. Stir in the beer, tomato paste, canned tomatoes, cumin, coriander, oregano, salt, black pepper, and hot sauce. Gently simmer, covered, for 15 minutes.

In another frying pan, heat the oil over moderately high heat. Add the potatoes and cook, stirring occasionally, until golden brown. Add the potatoes, raisins, and olives to the meat mixture. Cook, covered, until the potatoes are just done, about 5 minutes longer. Dehydrate at 160° until completely dry (about 8 hours). Cool and store in a large freezer baggie.

On the trail:

Add the picadillo to a large pot and barely cover with water. Place lid on pot and bring to a boil. Turn off stove and let sit until dehydrated (about 90 minutes). Add more water and reheat if needed. Serve with tortillas and extra hot sauce.

Corn and Black Bean Quesadillas

Who doesn't like quesadillas? Just don't forget your foldable spatula.
Makes 1 serving

You'll need:

Filling: ¾ cup freeze–dried or dehydrated corn
¾ cup freeze–dried or dehydrated black beans
1 t chili powder
1 t ground cumin
¼ t onion powder
1 t dried cilantro (optional)
2 packets True Lime (optional)

1 cup shredded (4 ounces) semi–hard cheese or cheese sticks
4 small tortillas (street–taco size works great)
Packets of hot sauce
Oil or ghee (stored in a leak–proof container)

At home:

Place all the filling ingredients into one baggie. Package the remaining ingredients as needed.

On the trail:

Freeze–dried foods rehydrate almost instantly. Dehydrated corn and beans take about 20 minutes to an hour, so plan accordingly. Add just enough water to the baggie of filling ingredients to fully rehydrate. Heat ghee or oil in a small skillet or the bottom of a pot. Add one tortilla; sprinkle with cheese; layer with filling ingredients; more cheese; and add the final tortilla layer. The cheese helps to 'glue' everything together.

Slowly heat until toasty on the bottom. Then press the top tortilla with the flat side of the spatula, and then *carefully* flip over. Cook until the other side of the tortilla is also toasty and the cheese has melted.

Street Tacos

Servings vary—the more people, the more fun toppings you'll want.

You'll need:
Corn or flour tortillas
Choice of protein(s):
- Dehydrated or freeze-dried beans, bean flakes or refried beans (page 75)
- Freeze–dried chicken or beef
- Shelf-stable pouches of salmon or chicken
- Smoked fish

Taco seasoning (packets or homemade, if needed)
Topping ideas:
- Dehydrated guacamole (page 69)
- Dehydrated salsa (pages 72 - 74) (and/or packets of hot sauce)
- Dehydrated sour cream powder or Greek yogurt
- Freeze–dried or dehydrated peppers, broccoli, asparagus, etc.
- Thinly sliced cabbage (this will keep a day or more, depending on weather)
- Pickled or fresh jalapeno peppers
- Grated cheese in bag (this will keep several days or freeze first)

Ghee or oil

At home:
You can buy canned or refried beans and dehydrate them yourself, or buy the 'instant' refried beans or flakes off–the–shelf. Package everything as needed, being sure to separate the protein from the toppings.

On the trail:
Add water to any bags that need rehydrating. Mix taco seasoning in protein bag, if needed. Heat ghee or oil in pan; add protein. Once hot, top with tortillas (to warm). Add toppings as desired.

Tamale Pie

A hearty, stick to your ribs kind of dinner.
4 large servings

You'll need for the filling:

¾ pounds *lean* ground beef (or soysage)
1 (14.5-ounce) can of crushed tomatoes
1 small can chopped green chiles
2 T tomato paste
½ t ground cumin
pinch of crushed red pepper
½ onion, chopped
½ red or green pepper, chopped
½ cup corn
1 large clove garlic, minced
1½ t chili powder
½ t salt

For the crust:

¾ cup Masa Harina (corn flour)
¾ t baking powder
½ t salt
¾ t chicken or veggie bouillon
1 T oil
Plus: 1 cup shredded cheddar cheese

At home:

For the filling: In a large skillet, brown the ground beef, along with the onion and green pepper. Add all the other ingredients. Bring to a low boil and then simmer for 5 minutes. Adjust seasonings, if necessary. Dehydrate on silicone fruit roll sheets at 160° until dry. Allow to cool, then store in a baggie.

Package the crust ingredients in a quart-sized freezer baggie; package the oil in a leak-proof bottle. Package the cheese as needed—a block of hard cheddar or a bag of shredded will keep on the trail for several days.

On the trail:

Add the filling ingredients to a pot or your baking pan. Cover with water; heat until hot; turn off the heat and cover; then allow to sit until thoroughly rehydrated. If the mixture looks too dry, you can add more water as needed. Reheat the mixture.

Add ¾ cup of water and the oil to the bag of crust ingredients. Massage the bag to mix well. If needed, add more water until you have a nice batter. Tear off one corner of the baggie and squeeze the batter over the top of the meat filling. Bake in a backpackers oven or a Fry-Bake pan until the crust is firm. Top with cheese.

If cooking in a pot, cook uncovered for 5 minutes. Cover and cook another 15 minutes. A hot water bath will create a cooked, but not crusty, topping. Alternately, you can fry corn cakes and top the meat filling with the cakes.

Spinach and Mushroom Enchiladas

A little dehydrating at home can make a tasty dinner out on the trail.
4 servings

You'll need:

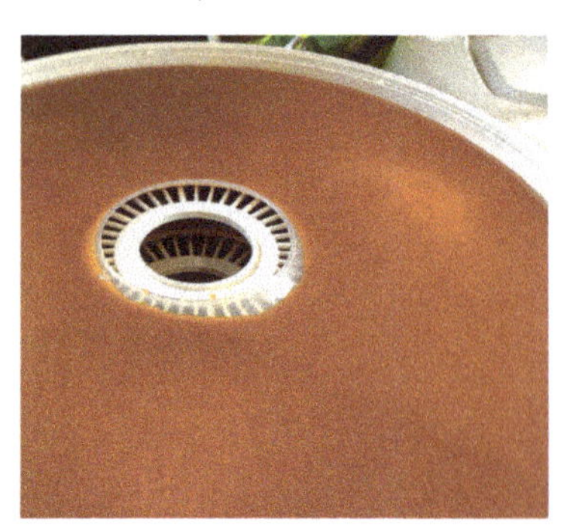

1 (28–ounce) can or homemade enchilada sauce
1 (12–ounce) bag frozen spinach
16 ounces fresh mushrooms, sliced or chopped
1 cup dehydrated refried beans (page 75)
1 t onion powder
1 t garlic powder
1 t ground cumin powder
8 or 12 (6–8") tortillas, flour or corn
Dry Parmesan or hard cheese (optional)

At Home:
Dehydrate the enchilada sauce, as you would spaghetti sauce (see page 76). Enchilada sauce can be quite thin; a 28–ounce can will easily cover two or three round silicone trays. Dehydrate at 135° until dry and then let cool. The enchilada sauce becomes like parchment paper and is easily crumbled. Divide the sauce in half; store one–half in a baggie and the other half in a second baggie to use another time.

Thaw the spinach and spread over a fine mesh tray. Dehydrate at 135° until thoroughly dried. Do the same for the mushrooms. You can buy already dried refried beans or simply take a can of your choice and dehydrate yourself. Place the spinach, mushrooms, refried beans, and spices in a second baggie. Package cheese as needed.

On the trail:
Add the dry enchilada sauce to a small pan. Add 1¼ cups water, heat until simmering, then turn off heat and let sit. Add the contents of the spinach mix baggie to a small pan. Add 4 cups water, heat until simmering, then turn off heat and let sit. Reheat if necessary to keep warm. Fill tortillas with the spinach mixture and top with enchilada sauce. Serve with Parmesan sprinkled on top.

Chicken Enchiladas

A little Tex–Mex and a little Southwest merge together in the backcountry.
4 servings

You'll need:
2 cups freeze–dried chicken (such as Honeyville's Rancher's Cut)
1 recipe Southwest Bean Salad, dehydrated (page 62)
½ recipe of dehydrated enchilada sauce (see facing page)
8 or 12 (6–8") tortillas, flour or corn

At Home:
Place the chicken in one baggie and the dehydrated Southwest Bean Salad in another baggie. Dehydrate the enchilada sauce, per the instructions on the facing page. Place one-half of the dehydrated sauce in a third baggie. Package the tortillas as needed.

On the trail:
Add one cup of water to the bag of Southwest Bean Salad and let rehydrate for one hour, adding more water if needed. Add one cup of water to the bag of freeze–dried chicken and let rehydrate for about ten minutes, adding more water if needed. Add the dry enchilada sauce to a small pot. Add 1¼cups of water, heat until simmering, then turn off heat and let sit.

Once the bean salad and the chicken are rehydrated, mix both in a small pot and gently heat. Once hot, place the tortillas on top of the chicken mixture, alternating the stack so that all the tortillas are warmed. (You can also do this in a small pan.) Roll the chicken and bean mixture in the tortillas and top with enchilada sauce. Olé!

Pizza and Calzones

Soooo good. You'll want everything prepped before you start baking.

You'll need:

Packet(s) of dry pizza dough mix, gluten–free, or homemade
Dehydrated pizza sauce (page 76) or pesto (page 82)
Toppings of choice: dehydrated peppers, mushrooms, and red onions; capers; smoked salmon; freeze–dried sausage; pepperoni; etc.
Cheese, such as smoked provolone, mozzarella, Romano, etc.
Extra packets of Parmesan cheese and red pepper flakes (optional)
Canola oil (packed in a plastic leak-proof bottle)

At Home:

Dehydrate your pizza sauce. Place all toppings in baggies (if needed). Buy already–grated cheese or bring a block along, using your pocket–knife to grate.

On the trail:

Add warm water to dough mix; lightly knead. We like to use small, collapsible silicone bowls so the dough does not stick. Cover dough and allow to rise (in a warm place, if possible).

Organize your toppings; rehydrate any sauce, veggies and meats by adding a little water to each bag. You want most ingredients moist, but not wet. Grate cheese if needed. Oil the baking pan.

Once the dough has risen, lightly oil or flour your fingers and spread dough in baking pan. You can also roll out the dough using a water bottle as a rolling pin. Spread pizza sauce or pesto over dough. Cover with cheese and toppings of choice.

Bake, using the backpackers oven or Banks Fry–Bake pan (pages 11 – 13). If using the Fry–Bake pan, be sure that your fire on top is very hot, with a very low heat on the bottom. Most pizzas and calzones take about 10 to 15 minutes to bake. If you can smell the pizza cooking, it may be getting overdone.

You can also bake using a heavy pan with a tight–fitting lid. If using any kind of fire–resistant dome shelter over your pan, be sure to use an external fuel bottle.

To make calzones, simply spread the dough across the entire bottom of the pan as previously indicated. Spread the sauce on one-half of the circle of dough. Distribute your toppings across the sauce and top with cheese. Then carefully fold over the other half of the dough on top and pinch the edges.

Making pizzas and calzones is not that hard. However, it's easy to practice at home until you get the hang of regulating the heat and the timing of everything. In fact, you can practice with fresh ingredients to make your life easier. Pick up a growler, invite a few friends over, and have a taste test right in your back yard. If anyone complains, it's their turn to cook.

Chicken Tikka Masala

An easy masala, using a full palette of flavors.
1 serving

You'll need:

¼ cup basmati rice, uncooked
⅛ t ginger powder
⅛ t turmeric powder
¼ t ground coriander
⅛ t cayenne
2 T dehydrated spaghetti sauce
1 T ghee or butter powder
1 packet True Lime
¼ t onion powder
¼ t salt / dehydrated cilantro
¼ t garam masala powder
⅛ t cumin
2½ t sour cream powder or dehydrated yogurt
1 T milk powder (NIDO)
½ to ⅔ cup freeze-dried chicken (or a 2.6–ounce, shelf–stable pouch)

At home:
Package all together, except for the ghee, True Lime, and chicken. Package those ingredients separately, as needed. Note: This has a little kick to it, so for a more tender palate, you may want to omit the cayenne.

On the trail:
Empty the contents of the rice bag and the ghee into a pot with 1½ cups water (do not add the chicken or True Lime yet.) If using a pouch of shelf–stable chicken, reduce the amount of water needed by ¼ cup. For freeze-dried chicken, add a few spoonfuls of water to the bag.

Bring the rice to a boil, cover, and reduce the heat to a simmer for 10 to 15 minutes, stirring occasionally. The rice should be wet, but not soupy. Add the chicken and True Lime; simmer another 5 minutes. Top with chopped wild onions or watercress, if available.

Panang Curry with Peanut Sauce

Easy to scale for a large group. Curry brands vary in terms of spiciness, so adjust accordingly.
1 serving

You'll need:

½ cup minute rice (brown or white)
¼ cup freeze-dried peas or mixed veggies
½ cup freeze-dried chicken (optional))
3 T powdered coconut milk
2 T (+/-) Panang curry powder
1 T powdered peanut butter
1 packet True Lime
½ t salt
1 T ghee (optional)

At home:

Dehydrate your own Panang or red curry paste on a fruit roll sheet (it is so worth it!) or use store–bought powder. Package all ingredients, except ghee, in a baggie.

On the trail:

Add dry ingredients, plus 1 cup water, to a pot. Bring to a boil, cover, then reduce the heat to a simmer for 5 minutes. Let sit for 5 minutes until everything is rehydrated (you can add more water, if needed). Mix in ghee and serve.

Tahini and Lemon–Ginger Noodles

The tahini imparts a rich–tasting depth to the flavor of the pasta. And you can easily sub other veggies for the mushrooms.
2 large servings

You'll need:
8 ounces thin pasta such as spaghetti, angel hair, somen or udon
8 ounces fresh mushrooms, sliced or chopped
2 t chili garlic sauce
3 t freshly grated ginger or 1½ t ground ginger
1 large garlic clove, minced
1 large lemon (or lime), zested and squeezed
2 t soy sauce or tamari
2 t olive oil
½ t salt
⅓ cup tahini (toasted ground sesame paste)
Extra packets of True Lemon or True Lime

At home:
Package the pasta as needed. Toss all the other ingredients into a small skillet. Cook over low heat until the mushrooms begin to brown and the aromatics intensify. Dehydrate the mushroom mixture at 135° until dry (4 to 5 hours). Cool and place in a separate baggie.

On the trail:
Add a little water to the mushroom mixture to begin the rehydration process. Cook the pasta until almost done. Then lightly toss with the mushroom mixture and heat through. Sprinkle with extra True Lemon or Lime powder for a livelier flavor.

Pad Thai

All this just barely fits into a 1.5 quart pot.
2 servings

Baggie #1: 1 red pepper, chopped and dehydrated
½ cup very thin strips of carrot, dehydrated
¾ cup freeze–dried broccoli
¾ cup freeze–dried chicken or dried shrimp (optional)
½ cup freeze–dried scrambled eggs (or make OvaEasy eggs at camp)

Baggie #2: ¾ t dried garlic flakes or powder
¾ t crushed red pepper
½ t ginger powder
2 or 3 T brown sugar
3 T peanut butter powder
4 True Lime packets
1 T dried cilantro (optional)
1 t ground dried shrimp (optional)

6 oz flat rice noodles (usually labeled as 'Pad Thai' noodles)
2 T soy sauce (4 to-go packets)
¼ cup chopped roasted peanuts

At home:
Organize baggies #1 and #2. Package the noodles, soy sauce, and peanuts separately.

On the trail:
1) Add just enough water to baggie #1 to begin rehydrating. You want things just moist.
2. Add the rice noodles to your pot (you may have to break in half) and barely cover with water. Heat to a low simmer.
3. Meanwhile, add the soy sauce packets to baggie #2 and combine well. If the sauce seems a bit too heavy, you can add a tablespoon or two of water.
4. Once the noodles are al dente, add baggie #1 to the pot. Only add more water if needed—it's best not to have to pour off any liquid. Gently mix and heat through. Then add baggie #2 to the pot. Gently mix well again and heat again.
5. Garnish with chopped peanuts (and wild green onions, if available).

Sushi Maki, Temaki and Poké Bowls

There are a few challenges to making sushi on the trail: First, while you can use instant or parboiled rice to reduce cooking time and fuel requirements, using actual sushi rice is infinitely better tasting. Second, you'll have to rely on a variety of store-bought ingredients, some of which have a limited trail life. Last, If you don't know how to make maki or hand rolls (temaki), YouTube is your friend. You can also bring a bamboo mat to help out or just wing it!

Items you'll need:
Sushi rice (such as Nishiki brand)
Japanese vinegar powder for sushi
Nori sheets
Packets of soy sauce or tamari
Pickled ginger (keeps well on the trail)
Wasabi powder or small tube of paste
Toasted sesame seeds (optional)

Basic fillings:
Tuna or salmon pouches such as Lemon Sesame & Ginger, or Spicy Thai Chili
Whole fresh avocado, stored in a large plastic Easter egg
English cucumber (an optional, but fresh, luxury item)

For Philly–style rolls:
Smoked salmon
Shelf–stable cream cheese
Cucumber strips

For spicy tuna/salmon rolls:
Tuna and/or salmon pouch
Mayo and hot sauce packets
Avocado slices

For futomaki rolls:
Pickled burdock root (Gobo)
Dried kanpyo (daikon radish)
Scrambled egg (OvaEasy)
Sakura Denbu (optional)
Whole carrot
Dried shiitake mushrooms, rehydrated on the trail
Any other fillings that sound good!

At Home:

Measure sushi rice, place in baggie, and label with cooking instructions. Most sushi rice is 1½ cups rice to 2 cups water. Select roll fillings from the list provided, or discover your own, and package as needed. Most Asian stores will carry these items.

On the trail:

Cook sushi rice as directed. (Soaking the rice in warm water will reduce the cooking time and save fuel.) Traditionally, after cooking sushi rice, it's sprinkled with a mixture of rice vinegar, sugar and salt; then gently tossed while it cools. You can either skip this step or use a ready–made vinegar powder. But the seasoning really makes the rice.

While the rice is cooking and cooling, prepare your other ingredients—slicing cukes or avocado; mixing salmon with mayo and hot sauce; making tamago (eggs); or prepping whatever else you brought along.

For sushi maki, use an entire sheet of nori. Spread the rice first and then place your fillings on one edge of the nori. If you want to get really fancy, make an inside–out roll. Sprinkle with sesame seeds; then garnish with pickled ginger and wasabi. Serve with soy sauce.

For temaki (pictured above), use only a half–sheet of Nori and fold cone shaped. Hand rolls are really easy to make out on the trail.

And Poké bowls are basically deconstructed sushi. Although a true sushi master would groan at all this, it sure tastes good to us after a day outdoors.

Favorite Homemade One-Pots

- Jambalaya
- Red Beans and Rice
- Creoles and Étouffées
- Chili (Cincinnati-style works great, too)
- Great Northern or Black Bean Soup
- Split Pea Soup
- Butternut Squash Soup

We have found that many of our favorite homemade soups and stews easily dehydrate and beautifully rehydrate out on the trail. You can cook up a big pot, dehydrate, and then store in the freezer until you're ready to use it. Or the next time you make a batch, dehydrate the leftovers for your next off the grid adventure.

Fresh chili on left; dehydrated on right.

A few words of advice: Use as little fat as possible; cut pieces into uniform sizes; shred or slice meat (if using) into thin pieces; fruit roll trays seem to work best for dehydrating most soups and stews; be careful with cream-based soups (you can always add NIDO or cheese when out on the trail); and warm the soup as it's dehydrating (to speed up the process). Thinner soups can also be made into 'fruit leather' style roll-ups, such as the roasted red pepper and pear soup (page 51).

Jambalaya, Artichoke & Parmesan Cream, and Chicken Creole from Bourbon n' Toulouse.

Don't cook much? No problem! Head to your local Cajun, Thai, Ethiopian or other favorite restaurant and pick-up an order to go. Even your neighborhood deli or grocery store has a good selection of homemade and packaged foods that work well. Simply dehydrate and enjoy out on the trail. Hey—if you don't tell, we won't either.

Tasty Dinner Hacks

Some nights you want to cook and impress your friends—and sometimes you want to hit the sack before the sun sets. Or this trip was a last minute thing, and you just didn't have time to pull dinner together. That's more than okay. Here are a few ideas, because none of us want to go to bed hungry.

- Zatarain's New Orleans–style mixes. Add freeze–dried sausage, a chicken pouch, or smoked sausage if desired.
- Any 'instant' rice or risotto mix, topped with freeze–dried or dehydrated veggies.
- Pasta, pesto (mix or homemade), loaded with freeze–dried or dehydrated veggies and/or meats.
- Tortellini and dehydrated spaghetti sauce, plus dried Parmesan cheese packets.
- Gnocchi (potato dumplings) (shelf–stable) with ghee, garlic, salt, and rosemary.
- Cornbread pancakes, made from just–add–water mix, to go with soups and stews.
- Falafel (just–add–water mix), pita, mayo and seasoning packets, and True Lime.
- Cornbread stuffing mix, freeze–dried chicken, and an optional packet of gravy mix. This makes a great lunch, too.
- Couscous (any flavor), with pine nuts and raisins. Or pecans and sun-dried tomatoes. Or grated Parmesan.
- Tuna or salmon pouches, served with hush–puppies (just–add–water mix).

Sweet Endings

Dessert is probably the most important stage of the meal,
since it will be the last thing your guests remember
before they pass out all over the table.

– William Powell

Black Forest Pudding

Quick and rich.
2 servings

You'll need:
4 T instant dark chocolate pudding mix (eg., Godiva)
4 T full cream milk powder (NIDO)
½ cup freeze–dried (or dried) sour cherries
8 fudge–covered chocolate cookies, 4 whole and 4 crumbled

At home:
Combine pudding and milk powders in a small baggie. Pack cherries and cookies of choice separately.

On the trail:
If using dried cherries, cover with water to rehydrate. Add the pudding and milk powders to a small bowl, along with a scant 1 cup of cold water. Alternately, you can add the water to the baggie of powders. Mix well. Stir in the cherries. Let the pudding rest to thicken. Meanwhile, when no one else is watching, eat the 4 whole cookies. Top the pudding with the remaining crushed cookies.

Gluten-free Chocolate Molten Lava Cakes

Decisively decadent.
8 servings

You'll need:
½ cup almond flour (meal)
½ cup gluten–free baking mix
5 T + 1 t (heaping ¼ cup) OvaEasy
5 T + 1 t (heaping ¼ cup) cocoa powder
½ cup sugar
1 t baking powder
¼ t of salt
½ cup semi-sweet chocolate chips
½ cup coconut oil
Silicone cupcake baking liners

At home:
Mix all the dry ingredients, including the chocolate chips, together in one large baggie. Put coconut oil in a separate bag or container.

On the trail:
Combine dry ingredients with coconut oil and 2 cups water. You can do this right in the baggie. Mix well, but do not over stir.

Spoon into silicone cups, being careful to equally distribute the chocolate chips. Nestle all the cups in one large pot or do them in two batches. Fill the pot with water until it reaches at least half or two–thirds up the sides of the silicone cups. See page 10 for more details on how to bake using a hot–water bath.

Cover the pot. Lightly boil for 20 minutes until cake is set. Check the water level to make sure the pot does not run dry. Cool slightly before removing cups from the hot water.

Gluten-free Apple Muffins

You can also substitute all–purpose flour for the gluten–free baking mix.
4 to 6 servings

You'll need:

½ cup almond flour (meal)
5 T + 1 t (heaping ¼ cup) OvaEasy
½ cup sugar
1 t baking powder
1 cup (freeze–)dried apples, chopped
Silicone cupcake baking liners
½ cup gluten–free baking mix
¼ cup instant oats
2 t ground cinnamon
¼ t salt
½ cup coconut oil

At home:

Mix all dry ingredients together. Put coconut oil in a separate bag or container.

On the trail:

Combine dry ingredients with coconut oil and 2 cups water. You can do this right in the baggie. Mix well, but do not over stir. Let sit for about 5 minutes.

Spoon into silicone cups, being careful to equally distribute the apples. Nestle all the cups in one large pot or do them in two batches. Fill the pot with water until it reaches at least half or two–thirds up the sides of the silicone cups. See page 10 for more details on how to bake using a hot–water bath.

Cover the pot. Lightly boil for 20 minutes until cake is set. Check the water level to make sure the pot does not run dry. Cool slightly before removing cups from the hot water.

Strawberry Rhubarb Crunch

You can easily substitute other fruits. Good for breakfast, too.
1 serving

You'll need:
3 T dehydrated or freeze–dried rhubarb
3 T dehydrated or freeze–dried strawberries
1 T sugar or other sweetener
⅓ cup crunchy granola

At home:
Freeze–dried rhubarb is hard to find. At this writing Honeyberry sells rhubarb pieces on Etsy. Freeze–dried strawberries are easily sourced. To keep rehydration times the same, it's best if both fruits are dried using the same method.

Dehydrating either fruit is easy—use tender (slender) rhubarb stalks cut to 1 inch in length or less. For 3 T dried rhubarb, you will need about 3 stalks. Strawberries should be sliced to uniform thickness. Dehydrate both at 135⁰ until leathery.

Mix fruit and sugar (if using) in a baggie. The sweetener helps mellow the tang of the rhubarb and makes more of a syrup that will absorb into the granola. Pack granola separately.

On the trail:
For dehydrated fruit: Dump fruit into a pan and add ⅓ cup water (you may need more water depending on fruit.) Place over medium heat; bring to a boil. Turn off heat and set pot aside (with lid and rock on top) for about 20 minutes, until the mixture is completely rehydrated.

For freeze–dried fruit: Add enough water to the baggie to cover the fruit. Allow to sit for 5 minutes.

If the fruit mixture is a little soupy, that's good. Serve over granola.

Angel Food Fruit Compote

Easy to make for a large group or scale back for yourself.
4 to 6 servings

You'll need:
1 store–bought angel food or pound cake (or make your own)
2 to 4 cups freeze–dried or dehydrated fruit of your choice
¼ cup sugar (optional)
1 (1.3) ounce packet whipped topping mix (eg., Dream Whip)
2 T full cream milk powder (NIDO)

At home:
Cube cake and dehydrate until dry (like croutons); place in baggie. Mix fruit and sugar in another baggie. Dump whipped topping and NIDO into another baggie. This is so good, you don't even need the Dream Whip.

On the Trail:
Sprinkle cake cubes with water—you don't need much, as the fruit syrup will rehydrate the cubes quite nicely. Place fruit, sugar and, 1 or 2 cups water in a pot and heat until fruit is fully rehydrated.

In general, dried fruit will require more water and longer to fully rehydrate, as compared to freeze–dried fruit. Add more water if needed to make it 'soupy'.

Add ½ cup cold water to whipped topping bag, seal, and shake vigorously for 3 to 4 minutes. Divide cake cubes and fruit mixture in bowls, then top with a dollop of whipped topping.

Any kind of cake dehydrates easily. Chocolate cake and dried cherries? Dried scones and peaches? This dessert can be rather bulky (but lightweight) to carry. But it's oh so worth the extra space!

Chow Mein Cherry Clusters

A nest of chocolate–covered chow mein noodles, with other goodies hidden inside.
8 clusters

You'll need:
1 cup semi–sweet chocolate chips (or a 6 ounce–slab of dark chocolate or carob)
½ cup dried or freeze–dried pitted, tart cherries*
½ cup pecans, coarsely chopped
½ cup slightly–broken, chow mein noodles**

Notes: *Considering dried versus freeze–dried cherries—each impart a different flavor to the clusters. The rehydrated freeze–dried cherries just *pop!* with flavor, while dried fruits are chewier and easier to transport. **You can also substitute thin pretzel sticks in lieu of the chow mein noodles.

At home:
Bag everything as needed, keeping the chocolate and the freeze–dried cherries (if using), bagged separately. Dried cherries can go into the same bag as the pecans and chow mein noodles.

On the trail:
If using freeze–dried cherries, lightly soak with water for about 30 minutes to rehydrate. Dried cherries can be used as is. Meanwhile, melt the chocolate in a small pan over a very low flame, stirring constantly. A tiny silicone spatula is perfect for stirring the chocolate.

Once the chocolate is melted, mix in all the other ingredients. Drop by large spoonfuls onto a flat surface (such as a plate or super–thin, plastic cutting board). Once fully cooled, the clusters will be ready to eat. If air temps are above 60⁰, the chocolate may not set up, rendering these finger–lickin' good.

You can experiment with other fruit and nut combinations, such as bananas chips and walnuts; craisins and slivered almonds; dried mango and cashews; or simply coconut.

Apple Caramel Crisp

Be on the lookout for the caramel notes! Tempting for breakfast, too.
1 serving

You'll need:
½ cup freeze–dried diced apples
3 T full cream milk powder (NIDO)
1 T instant vanilla pudding powder
½ T sugar
¼ t ground cinnamon
2 oatmeal cookies or ⅓ cup granola

At home:
Combine apples, milk powder, vanilla powder, sugar, and cinnamon in a small baggie. Pack crumbled oatmeal cookies or granola separately.

On the trail:
Dump apple mixture into a pot and add ½ cup cold water, stirring as you go. Place over medium heat and bring to a slow boil, stirring frequently. If using dried fruits, remember to allow for a little extra water and cooking time.

Reduce the heat and simmer a few minutes. Remove from heat and cool. Top with crushed cookies or crunchy granola.

Obviously you can substitute other fruits, pudding flavors, and kinds of cookies. Once again, recipes are basically a demonstration of technique or methodology, and the creativity is all your own!

Tiramisu

Versions of this recipe have been circulating on the Internet for several years. I have no idea who to thank. It is simply brilliant.
4 servings

You'll need:
16 ladyfinger biscuits, dry or dehydrated
1 small box instant vanilla pudding
1/2 cup full cream milk powder (NIDO)
1 packet instant coffee or espresso (such as Cafe Bustelo or Starbucks Via)
4 T Amaretto, Kahlua, rum, cognac, or similar liquor (optional)
Cocoa powder or dark chocolate for curling

Notes: You can omit the alcohol all together or sprinkle it on individual portions. You can also use Bird's custard powder (see page 146) in lieu of the instant vanilla pudding.

At home:
You can buy lady fingers that are 'dry' (such as Delallo or Alessi Biscotti Savoiardi). Alternately, you can buy them 'fresh' and easily dehydrate them yourself on trays.

Combine pudding and milk powders in one baggie. Pack the biscuits, instant coffee, liquor (plastic airline–style bottles work well) and chocolate separately.

On the trail:
Bring ⅓ cup water to a boil. Mix the hot water with instant coffee and set aside to cool. Mix pudding and milk powders with 2 cups cold water, directly in the baggie. Agitate for about 2 minutes, until pudding thickens. Stir in Amaretto liquor. Mix again and set aside.

Break 4 ladyfingers in half and place in a bowl. Repeat for 4 bowls. Drizzle one–half of the coffee over the 4 bowls. Spread one–half of the vanilla custard over the 4 bowls of ladyfingers. Repeat with a second layer. To serve, dust with cocoa powder or chocolate curls.

Peanut Butter Cream Pie

It's amazing how 'peanut butter' in the name of a pie can make you think it's healthy.
6 servings

You'll need:
12 peanut butter cookies (such as Nutter Butter) to make 1½ cups coarse crumbs
1 (11.1–ounce) box instant cheesecake mix
⅓ cup full cream milk powder (NIDO)
⅓ cup pure powdered peanut butter (with no added sugar)

At home:
Place the cookies in a small baggie. Combine cheesecake mix, powdered milk, and powdered peanut butter in a separate baggie. Discard the graham cracker pouch that came with the mix or save for another use.

On the trail:
Store the bag of cookies in the bottom of your pack for three or four days—or break the cookies in the baggie until crumbly. Press into the bottom of your largest pan or pot (a 9" diameter works great), withholding about 1 or 2 tablespoons of crumbs. Heat over a low flame until the crust is lightly toasted, about 2 to 3 minutes, then cool.

In a separate pot or bowl, combine the cheesecake, milk powder, and powdered peanut butter with 1½ cups of cold water. Beat well for 4 to 5 minutes, until creamy and fluffy.

Spread the cheesecake on top of the crust. Top with the remaining crumbs. The filling sets up fairly quickly, but it's good to let sit for at least 10 minutes before gorging.

This pie is so rich it could easily be stretched to 8 servings, although some might argue.

Key Lime Pie

As Bear tells us 'A slice a day, keeps scurvy at bay.'
6 servings

You'll need:
1 (11.1–ounce) box instant cheesecake mix
¼ c ghee (or coconut oil)
⅓ cup full cream milk powder (NIDO)
5 packets of True Lime for subdued excitement; 10 packets for a zesty taste

At home:
Place the graham cracker crumbs and ghee in a small baggie. Combine cheesecake mix, powdered milk, and True Lime in a separate baggie.

On the trail:
Massage the graham cracker and ghee in the baggie until crumbly. Press into the bottom of your largest pan or pot (a 9" diameter works great). Heat over a low flame until the crust is lightly toasted. Let cool. In a separate pot or bowl, combine the cheesecake mix with 1½ cups of cold water. Beat well for 4 to 5 minutes, until creamy and fluffy. Spread the cheesecake on top of the crust. Let sit for at least 15 minutes before devouring.

Grand Portage Mud Pie

So simple. So rich. And definitely worth portaging for.
6 servings

You'll need:
1 (11.1–ounce) box instant cheesecake mix
⅓ cup full cream milk powder (NIDO)
2 or 3 T unsweetened dark cocoa powder
12 Oreo–style cookies + small dark chocolate bar

At home:
Combine cheesecake mix, powdered milk, and cocoa in a baggie. Place Oreo cookies in a separate baggie. Save graham cracker crust pouch for another use.

On the trail:
Break Oreos in the baggie until crumbly. Press crumbs into the bottom of your largest pan or pot (a 9" diameter works great). In a separate pot or bowl, combine the cheesecake mix with 1½ cups of cold water. Beat well for 4 to 5 minutes, until creamy and fluffy. Spread the cheesecake on top of the crust. With your pocket knife, shave chocolate curls over the top. Let sit for at least 15 minutes before diving in!

Grasshopper Pie

Might be better than chocolate–covered grasshoppers....
6 servings

You'll need:
1 (11.1–ounce) box instant cheesecake mix
1½ cups fudge–enrobed mint chocolate cookie crumbs (think GS Thin Mints)
⅓ cup full cream milk powder (NIDO)
1 or 2 t pure mint extract, depending on taste (*see note below*)
8 or so Andes Mints

At home:
The easiest way to make cookie crumbs at home is to put the cookies in a small baggie and crush with a rolling pin; or use a water bottle or flat rock at camp. Save the graham cracker crust pouch from the cheesecake mix for another use.

Combine the cheesecake mix and powdered milk in a separate baggie. You can carry the mint extract in it's own small plastic bottle. Note: *Real* grasshopper pie uses creme de menthe liqueur and white creme de cacao. The choice is yours.

On the trail:
In an 8 or 9–inch pot or pan, add the cookie crumbs and press with the back of a spoon to form the crust. In a bowl or small pot, combine the cheesecake mix with 1½ cups of cold water. Add the mint extract and mix well. Beat for 4 to 5 minutes, until creamy and fluffy. Pour the mix into your crust— it sets up fairly quickly.

Chop Andes mints and if available, top with a real sprig of fresh mint. We are roughing it... right?

Lemon Meringue Pie

You can make pies in your skillet, a pot, or individual bowls and mugs.
6 servings

You'll need:
1 (11.1)–ounce box instant cheesecake mix
1½ cups Meyer Lemon Shortbread or lemon sandwich cookies
⅓ cup full cream milk powder (NIDO)
8 or 10 packets of True Lemon
1 (1.3 ounce) packet whipped topping mix (eg., Dream Whip)
2 T full cream milk powder (NIDO)

At home:
The easiest way to make cookie crumbs at home is to put the cookies in a small baggie and crush with a rolling pin; or use a water bottle or flat rock at camp. Save the graham cracker crust pouch from the cheesecake mix for another use. Combine the cheesecake mix, ⅓ cup powdered milk, and True Lemon in a separate baggie. Place the Dream Whip and 2 T powdered milk in the last baggie. Note: The whipped topping is totally optional.

On the trail:
In an 8 or 9–inch pot or pan, add the cookie crumbs and press with the back of a spoon to form the crust. The gooey part of the sandwich cookie helps to hold the crust together. In a bowl or small pot, combine the cheesecake mix with 1½ cups of cold water. Beat for 4 to 5 minutes, until creamy and fluffy. Pour the mix into your crust— it sets up fairly quickly.

Add ½ cup cold water to the whipped topping bag, seal, and shake vigorously for 3 to 4 minutes. Cut the tip off the baggie and carefully squeeze the whipped topping over the pie. Let sit for a few minutes and then serve.

Ginger Cheesecake

Feel free to tone down the spices in this one, unless you want the full experience.
6 servings

You'll need:
1 (11.1–ounce) box instant cheesecake mix
1½ cups ginger snap crumbs (or Trade Joe's Triple Ginger) (about 16, 2" cookies)
¼ c ghee (or coconut oil)
⅓ cup full cream milk powder (NIDO)
¼ t ground nutmeg
½ t ground cardamom
½ t ground cinnamon
½ t ground allspice
½ t ground coriander

At home:
Place cookie crumbs and ghee in a small baggie. Combine the cheesecake mix, powdered milk, and remaining spices in a separate baggie. Save the graham cracker crust pouch for another use.

On the trail:
In a large pot or pan, add the cookie crumbs and ghee; press with the back of a spoon to form the crust. Heat gently over a low flame until the crust is toasty, then cool. You can also press the crust into individual bowls or mugs.

In a bowl or small pot, combine the cheesecake mix with 1½ cups of cold water. Beat for 4 to 5 minutes, until creamy and fluffy. Pour the mix into your crust— it sets up fairly quickly.

Bananas Flambé

We think anyone who likes the outdoors might also like to play with fire.
4 servings

You'll need:

#1: 1 cup of freeze–dried bananas (or fruit of your choice)
#2: 2 T brown sugar
¼ t ground cinnamon
#3: 1 small box instant vanilla pudding
1/2 cup full fat milk powder (NIDO)
⅓ cup ghee
⅓ to ½ cup dark rum or bourbon (preferably 100 proof)
2 T coarsely chopped pecans (optional)

At home:
Place the fruit in one baggie. Combine the brown sugar and the cinnamon in a second baggie. Combine the pudding powder and the NIDO in a third baggie. Pack the ghee and the alcohol in leak–proof bottles. Pack the pecans separately, if using.

On the trail:
Add 2 cups of cold water to the pudding and milk powder baggie. Agitate for about 2 minutes, mixing well, until pudding thickens. Set aside. Sprinkle the bananas with a little bit of water—they should dehydrate fairly quickly, but you do not want them mushy.

In a pan, melt the ghee. Add the brown sugar and the cinnamon, stirring until the sugar dissolves. Add the bananas and heat through. Turn off the burner and remove the pan from the heat. Pour the rum or bourbon over the hot mixture and safely ignite (while the mixture is still hot). The alcohol should burn off rather quickly, leaving lots of good flavor. Serve over vanilla pudding. Sprinkle with pecans, if desired.

Royal Chocolate Golden Lion

A warm custard, swirled with dark chocolate. Based on a very old recipe from Boone Tavern, Berea, Kentucky.
4 servings

You'll need:
2 T Bird's custard powder
2 T sugar (or other powdered sweetener)
1/2 cup full cream milk powder (NIDO)
Dark chocolate bars or chocolate truffles

At home
Place the dry ingredients in a small baggie. Package your chocolate of choice separately.

On the trail:
Empty the contents of the baggie into a small pot. Add about ¼ cup water and stir into a gooey paste.

Place over medium–low heat and slowly add about 1½ cups water, mixing as you go. Heat the custard, stirring frequently if not constantly, with a small whisk or silicone spatula, until the custard just begins to lightly boil.

Carefully pour the hot custard into bowls or mugs. Top with chocolate. As the chocolate melts, gently swirl but do not mix entirely. You want the flavor of the warm custard, mixed with distinct tastes of chocolate. How much chocolate you add is up to you.

Alfred Bird created this instant custard powder in the United Kingdom, circa 1837, because he was allergic to eggs (a primary ingredient in most custards). Bird's remains popular the world over, particularly amongst vegetarians, vegans, and busy cooks.

(Almost) Nanaimo Bars

This recipe is rather complicated for the backcountry. A small silicone spatula to spread the layers helps immensely. Or just make individual servings in small mugs or bowls. Makes 12 servings

You'll need:

For the crust:
- 2 T sugar
- 3 T unsweetened cocoa powder
- 1 T OvaEasy egg crystals (optional)
- ½ cup graham crackers crumbs
- ¼ finely chopped almonds (or pecans)
- ⅓ cup coconut flakes
- ⅓ c ghee or coconut oil

For the filling:
- 1 T Bird's custard powder
- 1 T full fat milk powder (NIDO)
- ¾ cup confectioner's sugar
- ¼ c ghee

For the topping:
- ¾ cup semi-sweet chocolate, chopped
- 1½ T ghee

Photo is only wishful thinking. My bars never, ever look this perfect!

At home:

Combine all the dry crust ingredients into one baggie; package the ghee or coconut oil separately. Combine all the dry filling ingredients into another baggie; package the ghee separately. Measure the chocolate into one small baggie; package the ghee separately. (If you're good at math, you can put all the ghee in one container.)

On the trail:

Crust: Heat ⅓ cup ghee or coconut oil in a pot or skillet. Once completely melted, mix in the dry crust ingredients. Mix well and then mix again. Pack in the bottom of that same pot or skillet, firmly pressing the crust down with the back of a spoon.

Filling: Add ¼ cup ghee, plus 1 T of water, to the baggie of filling ingredients. Massage vigorously. Add another 1 T of water if the filling is too thick. Spread over the top of the crust. Let set up.

Topping: Melt 1½ T ghee and the chocolate together. Carefully spread over the filling. Allow to completely cool— if possible, chilling is even better.

Named in the early 1950s after Nanaimo, BC, the history of these bars remains elusive.

Free Range Fruitcake

A big shout-out to Alton Brown for this inspiration!
4 large muffins

You'll need:
2 cups dried (not candied!) fruit such as:
½ cup golden raisins
½ cup currants
¼ cup dried cranberries
¼ cup prunes, diced
¼ cup dried cherries, diced
¼ cup dried apricots, diced
2 T natural crystallized ginger, diced
Zest of 1 lemon and 1 orange, dried
½ cup rum (or one pouch of instant apple cider mix)
⅛ t ground cloves
⅛ t ground allspice
¼ t ground cinnamon
½ cup sugar
4 T (¼ cup) ghee
¾ cup all-purpose flour
½ t salt
½ t baking powder
½ t baking soda
2 T OvaEasy egg crystals
⅓ cup chopped pecans

At home:
Place the dried fruit, ginger and zest in a small baggie.
Package the rum; spices and sugar; and ghee separately. Finally, put the last 6 dry ingredients into their own bag.

On the trail:
Place all the dried fruit, ginger, and zest in one pot. Add the rum and heat to a simmer. If using the cider mix, add it in lieu of the rum, plus ½ cup water. After simmering a few minutes, turn off the heat and let the fruit and rum mixture cool.

Add the spices, sugar, and ghee to the pot, along with ½ cup water. Bring to a low boil and simmer a few more minutes. Off heat, add the last bag of dry ingredients and mix gently. Place in 4 silicone baking cups and follow the directions on page 10 for baking in a hot water bath. The muffins should be done in about 20 minutes.

Strawberry Spoon Cake

Another take off an old-timey recipe. You can use gluten-free baking mix instead of the flour or any other fruit such as peach, mango or blueberry.
4 to 6 servings

You'll need:
1 ounce freeze-dried strawberries or 1½ cup dehydrated strawberries
1 T sugar
1 packet True Lemon
½ cup all-purpose flour
½ cup whole wheat flour
¼ cup brown sugar
½ t baking powder
¼ t baking soda
¼ t salt
2 T full cream milk powder (NIDO)
1 T ghee or oil

At home:
Place the strawberries, sugar and True Lemon in one baggie. Place all the other dry ingredients in a second baggie. Package the ghee or oil in a leak-proof bottle.

On the trail:
Pour a scant ½ cup of water into the baggie of strawberries. Allow to rehydrate. Add ½ cup water to the baggie of dry ingredients. Massage/mix well.

You can bake this using any of the options found on pages 10 through 12. If using the fry-bake pan, heat the ghee or oil over your stove. Squeeze the batter into the pan; hollow out a shallow area in the center of the batter to hold the strawberries (pictured top right).

Bake using the lowest heat setting of your stove and a twig fire or bed of coals on the lid. After 6 to 8 minutes, turn off the stove. Allow to bake another 6 to 8 minutes using only the top heat. Serve warm. Also good for breakfast.

No-Bake Cookies

A mid-century modern cookie from the 1960s.
Makes about 16 balls or cookies.

You'll need:
¼ cup ghee
¾ cup brown sugar (or ½ c honey)
2 T unsweetened cocoa or carob powder
1 T full cream milk powder (NIDO)
¼ cup unsweetened peanut butter powder
1¾ quick-cooking oats

At home:
Package the ghee (and honey, if using) in a leak-proof bottle. Place the sugar, cocoa or carob, NIDO, and peanut butter powder in one baggie and the oats in a second baggie.

On the trail:
Melt the ghee (and honey, if using) in a medium-sized pot. Mix in the sugar, cocoa, NIDO and peanut butter powder. Add ¼ cup water and combine well. Slowly stir in the oats until well-blended. Allow to sit until cool to the touch.

Roll into balls and, if desired, flatten into cookies using your thumb or the back of a spoon. These things can leave your hands a bit sticky, which may be a problem or a delightful opportunity.

Sweet Mango Custard

You can substitute any fruit, freeze–dried or dehydrated.
4 servings

You will need:
1 ounce freeze–dried mangoes, lightly crushed
6 T full cream milk powder (NIDO)
¼ cup OvaEasy whole egg crystals
¼ cup sugar or other sweetner
Pinch each of salt and nutmeg or cinnamon

At home:
Combine all the ingredients into one baggie. One cup of dehydrated fruit can be substituted for the freeze–dried, but should be partially rehydrated before baking. Be sure to pack 4 silicone baking cups.

On the trail:
Add 1¼ cup water to the baggie; massage gently, but thoroughly. Let rest for 5 minutes while you assemble the cookware. Carefully distribute the mango and custard mix into the 4 silicone baking cups.

Using the instructions on page 10, bake the custard in a hot water bath for 15 minutes or so. You don't need a hard boil—a soft boil works just as well and saves fuel. Be careful lifting the lid off the pot so that the condensation does not drip into the cups. When done, the tops of each custard cup will bounce back slightly. Allow to cool. This makes a very light and silky egg custard.

Avocado Black Bean Brownies

You can also dehydrate the beans and avocado, substitute OvaEasy for the eggs, and package all the other ingredients to bake on the trail. A backpacker's oven or Fry-Bake pan make this easy to do. Or just make them at home—either way these bars are yum!

You'll need:

1 can (15 oz) black beans, drained (or about 1½ cups cooked beans)
½ of a large ripe avocado (or one whole small avocado)
2 large eggs
1 T melted coconut or other vegetable oil
½ cup unsweetened cocoa powder
½ t baking powder
¼ t baking soda
¼ t salt
1 t pure vanilla extract
⅔ cup coconut or brown sugar
½ cup chocolate chips + 2 T for topping
½ cup chopped nuts (optional)

At home:

Preheat oven to 350°. Lightly oil an 8x8 inch baking pan. Place all ingredients (except chocolate chips) into a food processor. Puree until a smooth batter is formed. Add ½ cup chocolate chips (including nuts, if using), and fold into batter.

Pour batter into baking pan and sprinkle with remaining chocolate chips. Bake for 25-35 minutes or until the top of the brownies begin to crack. Cool pan completely before cutting.

To take on the trail, carefully cut into bars and individually wrap as needed. To prolong trail life, you can freeze the bars first.

Tasty Dessert Hacks

- You can't go wrong with s'mores—marshmallows, graham crackers and chocolate.
- Any instant pudding, best made with NIDO milk powder.
- Banana pudding? Nilla wafers, banana/vanilla pudding and freeze–dried 'nanas.
- A good mug of deep rich hot chocolate, with a dash of cayenne added for some kick. Mmmm.
- Any just–add–water muffin or brownie mix made into skillet cookies or muffins (using the silicone cups described on page 10).
- A small box of rich chocolates from your favorite chocolatier.
- Freeze a tube of ready–made cookie dough (thaws in a day or two). Slice and fry in skillet (no oil needed).
- Granola bar topped with almond butter from a pouch.
- Warm apple cider from a packet, dressed up with ginger, cinnamon and cloves.
- Sweet cinnamon rolls (in a can from the dairy case), wrapped around a stick, and cooked over the fire. Drizzle with the icing if you really need the empty calories.
- Tortilla generously smeared with Nutella, folded in half, and toasted in skillet.
- Ritz crackers dipped in melted Andes mint chocolates (aka GS Thin Mints).
- Irish coffee (hot coffee, Irish whiskey, sugar, and Dream Whip).

About the Author

Valerie Askren is the author of several books, including *Hike the Bluegrass and Beyond*; *Fly Fishing Kentucky*; *Backpacking Kentucky*; and *Five Star Trails: Louisville and Southern Indiana.* An avid outdoorswoman, Valerie has swum in Africa's Lake Malawi, climbed China's Mount Tai, sailed the coast of France, biked Nova Scotia, and backpacked the West Coast Trail of Vancouver Island. Her honeymoon was spent kayaking the Grand Canyon with her husband, Ben. The mother of four, Valerie lives in Lexington, Kentucky.

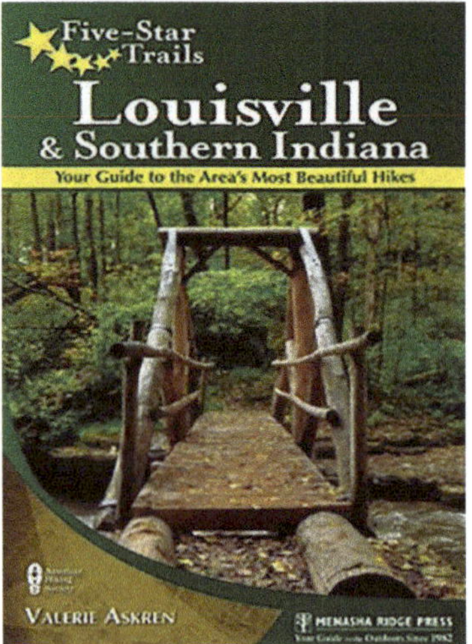

www.ingramcontent.com/pod-product-compliance
Lightning Source LLC
LaVergne TN
LVHW052346100826
845147LV00012B/761

* 9 7 8 1 7 3 7 8 1 5 6 0 0 *